You Are Not Alone

REST AND REFUGE FOR SPOUSAL CAREGIVERS

You Are Not Alone

REST AND REFUGE FOR SPOUSAL CAREGIVERS

Linda Waltersdorf Cobourn, EdD

Carpenter's Son Publishing

You Are Not Alone: Rest and Refuge for Spousal Caregivers

Published by Carpenter's Son Publishing, Franklin, Tennessee
www.carpenterssonpublishing.com

Edited by Jill B. Wilson

Cover and Interior Design by Suzanne Lawing

ISBN: 978-1-968127-35-0 (print)

Printed in the United States of America

Contents

Invisible but Never Alone

Let us not become weary in doing good,
for at the proper time, we will reap a harvest
if we do not give up. (Galatians 6:9)

This is a true confession from me to you. There were many times I desperately wanted to give up my role as a spousal caregiver. Often, only the vow I made before Ron and God at the marriage altar kept me from walking away.

For almost two decades of my husband's illness, I lived under an avalanche of adjectives. Some described our challenging situation: exhausting, exasperating, dirty, smelly, depressing, time-consuming, soul-crushing, and never-ending. Other adjectives described how I felt in the situation: worn-out, anxious, helpless, invisible.

Yes, I felt invisible, a feeling I found troublesome.

I was a member of a faith community, the same one where Ron and I had served for many years while raising our three children. Yet no one seemed concerned with how this wife, mother of three, caregiver, and full-time teacher was faring. Every Sunday, members of our church asked, “How is Ron?” But only my closest friends wanted to know how I was doing under the crushing weight of so many responsibilities once shared with my husband.

Unfortunately, feeling unnoticed while caring for an ill spouse is not unusual. According to the National Institute on Aging, 40 to 70 percent of the over five million spousal caregivers in the United States report often feeling isolated or depressed. While the Well Spouse Association (Wellspouse.org) offers some community, there are only twenty-two support groups nationwide.

Studies referenced on the Well Spouse website show that caring for a spouse is more medically intensive and lasts longer than caring for other family members, such as parents.

Providing $470 billion in uncompensated care, spousal caregivers grapple with finances and with the development or exacerbation of their own health challenges. Yet, spousal caregivers are a largely invisible social demographic.

After years of caring for my husband, I know how heavy the loneliness and invisible weight of caregiving can feel. But Psalm 91 reminds us we are never hidden from God's sight. His faithfulness is our shelter, his presence our covering.

We are seen, known, and held by God.

My journey as a caregiver for my husband, who had both physical and mental impairments, spanned nineteen years. After Ron died in 2019, that caregiving ended, but my burden for others walking the same rocky path did not.

If spousal caregiving is part of your journey, I long for you to know you are not alone. Even when you feel invisible to surrounding people, you are never invisible to God. Second Corinthians 4:16–18 encourages us to continue a challenging journey while looking to God, who always sees us. *Therefore, we do not lose heart. Though outwardly we are wasting away, yet inwardly we are being renewed day by day. For our light and momentary troubles are achieving for us an eternal glory that far outweighs them all. So we fix our eyes not on what is seen, but on what is unseen, since what is seen is temporary, but what is unseen is eternal.*

God sees you. God knows you. And while your human body—and heart—may grow weary as you walk this path, God can and will give you the strength, encouragement, and support you need.

God's Psalm 91 promises are for you. Believers don't get to skip the hard stuff. You're probably reading this study because life seems tough right now. Perhaps your loved one is in the hospital or ill. If you're finding it difficult to keep a positive outlook through discouraging situations or circumstances, I understand. I've been there.

No matter what my situation, I've found comfort in Psalm 91. While the Bible does not tell us who authored Psalm 91, it has been called the most cheering and positive of the psalms. Clear throughout its sixteen lines are God's promises, presence, power, protection, and provision for those who face distressing circumstances and seek refuge in him.

I pray you, too, will find comfort in this powerful psalm's lines.

Psalm 91

Whoever dwells in the shelter of the Most High,
will rest in the shadow of the Almighty.
I will say of the Lord, "He is my
refuge and my fortress,
my God in whom I trust."
Surely he will save you from the fowler's snare
and from the deadly pestilence.
He will cover you with his feathers,
and under his wings you will find refuge;
his faithfulness will be your shield and rampart.
You will not fear the terror of the night,
nor the arrow that flies by day,

nor the pestilence that stalks in the darkness,
nor the plague that destroys at midday.
A thousand may fall at your side,
ten thousand at your right hand,
but it will not come near you.
You will only observe with your eyes
and see the punishment of the wicked.
If you say, "The Lord is my refuge,"
and you make the Most High your dwelling,
no harm will overtake you,
no disaster will come near your tent.
For he will command his angels concerning you,
to guard you in all your ways.
They will lift you up with their hands,
so that you will not strike your foot against a stone.
You will tread on the lion and the cobra;
you will trample the great lion and the serpent.
"Because he loves me," says the Lord,
"I will rescue him;
I will protect him because he
acknowledges my name.
He will call on me, and I will answer him;
I will be with him in trouble,
I will deliver him and honor him.
With long life will I satisfy him
and show him my salvation."

The Sacred Caregiving Journey

You have embarked on the sacred journey of caregiving. On your journey, you will be stretched in ways you never expected. But you do not walk the journey alone.

Your caregiving road may be long, but God's faithfulness will carry you through. As you move forward through this study, you will be invited to

Rest in the shelter of God's protection,

Renew your weary soul in his Word, and

Remember all he has done and promises to do for you.

This study was created with you—the weary, faithful, and often time-stretched caregiver—in mind. Each chapter includes a short *"Take a Moment"* reflection. These are designed to meet you right where you are, offering a brief space to pause, breathe, and connect with God's presence and promises. I encourage you to make time for these moments whenever you can.

You'll also find a few additional questions and optional exercises in each chapter. These go a little deeper by inviting you to explore more of what Psalm 91 has to say to your heart and your unique caregiving journey. If you're able, I hope you'll engage with these too. They're not meant to add weight, but to help lift some of the load you carry, by rooting you more deeply in God's Word.

Whether you do a little or a lot, whether you write out your answers or just think them through in a quiet moment, this study is here to walk with you—not rush you. Go at your own pace and let the Holy Spirit guide your steps.

When you are ready to begin, please meet me in Chapter 1. It will be helpful to have a pen or pencil, so you can complete the activities intended to help you apply what you read to your personal journey.

CHAPTER 1

Sheltering in God's Shadow

Verse for the Journey: Whoever dwells in the shelter of the Most High will rest in the shadow of the Almighty. (Psalm 91:1)

From Linda's Journey

March 2, 2000

8:00 p.m.

It is a clear night; the moon and the stars shimmer against the velvet sky, beacons of hope. My daughter and I cross the street to where her car is parked, the streetlights casting shadows on the black road. I feel as if I'm floating, suspended between time and space.

Put one foot in front of the other, I tell myself. Keep walking. Keep breathing. This is not real. I slide into Bonnie's red Taurus. This cannot be happening.

A photograph from my wedding album flashes into my mind. Ron, so tall and strong in his powder-blue tuxedo, holds my hand as we leave the church, my white veil billowing around us. We pause for the camera. He turns and smiles at me, his eyes shining with love.

How did we get from that moment of promise to here?

Oh. A bad car accident. That's how.

Bonnie turns the key in the ignition. Headlights cut through the night. A cocoon of protection envelops us. Perhaps we can just stay here, driving forever in the night and never arriving at the trauma unit where Ron is in surgery, his life in the balance.

I lean my head back against the passenger seat. My thoughts and emotions are scattered. Will Ron live? Will he fully recover? What will life be like now? I am numb, but I know everything hinges on this moment. Everything will change.

I am not strong enough to do it on my own. I will need to remain sheltered in God's shadow, walking with him.

Rest in God's Protection

Chances are, my friend, you haven't had a lot of rest lately. Maybe your loved one is in the hospital. Maybe you're managing a household, a job, kids, meals, medications, bills—trying to hold yourself together. Perhaps this season of caregiving is new and came on suddenly, or maybe it's been building slowly.

Either way, chances are you're tired.

Take a moment here to stay in God's shadow, letting his love cover you. For the next five minutes, find a comfortable chair or at least a more comfortable position. Dwell in the shelter of the Most High. Resting in the shadow of God will not remove the weight of caregiving, but will give your soul a space of peace.

The Bible describes God's shadow as a place of refuge, like the cool shade beneath a mighty tree on a scorching day. Psalm 27:5 paints a similar picture of the safety offered in his shadow. Pen in hand, underline or highlight words in the verse that denote places where we might rest in God's care.

For in the time of trouble he shall hide me in his pavilion: in the secret of his tabernacle shall he hide me; he shall set me up upon a rock.

God promises to protect you. He will keep you safe in his dwelling, hide you in his tent, and place you so high on a rock that no harm will come near you. To rest in God's shadow is to rest in his protection. You can stay there until you are ready to face the world again.

According to Webster's Dictionary, the verb dwell means "to live as a resident." To dwell is not just to visit in times of trouble. God invites you to live with him always, safe in his care. God's shadow isn't fixed in one place; it moves with you through the various tasks of caregiving.

Have you ever walked so close to someone that your shadows merged? That's what walking with God is like. Even at noon, when the sun is high and your own shadow disappears, God's shadow remains.

Life may feel overwhelming right now, but God will always walk with you. He will also send others to help you on the journey.

Who will walk in God's shadow alongside you? As you write here the names of people you think of, pray that they will remain sheltered in God's shadow.

___

___

___

Renew Through God's Word

The weariness of caregiving calls for spiritual renewal. Reading Scripture is a powerful source of renewal. When you are exhausted, God's Word can bring you into his presence, where you can remain sheltered in his shadow. The Bible explores four images of God's protective shadow.

The Shadow of His Rock

Each one will be like a shelter from the wind and a refuge from the storm, like streams of water in the desert and the shadow of a great rock in a thirsty land. (Isaiah 32:2)

God's shadow is cool, solid, and unmoving. When everything in your life feels chaotic, he is your rock. Picture a massive boulder in a river. The water moves around it, but the rock stays put.

What image comes to your mind when you read Isaiah 32:2? Use this space to draw or describe it.

The Shadow of His Tree

Like an apple tree among the trees of the forest, is my beloved among the young men. I delight to sit in his shade, and his fruit is sweet to my taste. (Song of Solomon 2:3)

You are God's beloved. He invites you to rest beneath the shade of his love and enjoy the sweetness he offers. Just as you might lean against a sturdy apple tree, you can lean on God.

List five adjectives you would use to describe an apple tree.

____

____

____

The Shadow of His Wings

Because you are my help, I sing in the shadow of your wings. (Psalm 63:7)

You might not want to sing right now. It's probably all you can do to put one foot in front of the other and keep moving ahead. But God is your helper. He gives you space to breathe, to rest, and to be sheltered.

Briefly write what you think it might feel like to be surrounded by God's wings.

____

____

____

____

____

____

The Shadow of His Hand

He made my mouth like a sharpened sword, in the shadow of his hand he hid me; he made me into a pol-

ished arrow and concealed me in his quiver. (Isaiah 49:2)

When you're too worn out to answer another question or make one more decision, God is willing to hide you gently in his hand. He has also been preparing you for this time. Facing hard and unexpected events has given you strength of character. You've learned practical skills from caring for and organizing family life. Painful seasons have taught you to offer comfort to others. God has placed friends, family, and members of your faith community to support you. God's Scripture has laid a foundation for you.

Think about where you are in life right now and where you have been. List one way God has prepared you for this time.

____

____

____

Remember God's Faithfulness

Spousal caregivers don't hear a lot of promises. Our lives are full of uncertainty. Will this medication cure the infection? Will the next surgery fix the pancreas? It can be hard to recognize God's promises in the middle of a hospital stay, an insurance call, or another interrupted night of sleep. Remembering how he has kept his promises in the past gives us hope for today.

God's promises are certain. His Word is full of promises, and he keeps every single one of them. Here are just a few.

Nothing Will Separate Us from His Love

No illness, no distance, no measure of time divides us from God. The world of a caregiver often spins out of control, but Romans 8:35 assures us that God still holds us tight.

Who shall separate us from the love of Christ? Shall trouble or hardship or persecution or famine or nakedness or danger or sword?

God Will Work Everything for Good

It may not always seem as if anything is working for good. Test results can be alarming, and mysterious illnesses arise. As our redeemer, God does not waste our pain. The way he addresses it may not be the way we expect, but Romans 8:28 tells us something good will come from all of our trials.

And we know that in all things God works for the good of those who love him, who have been called according to his purpose.

We Can Have Peace

During Ron's many hospitalizations, inner peace was often difficult for me to find. Finding peace in a hospital ICU was a challenge, but I realized that I needed to keep my focus on Jesus, not on the circumstances. John 14:27 describes the peace God grants as something outside of our expectations.

Peace I leave with you; my peace I give you. I do not give to you as the world gives. Do not let your hearts be troubled and do not be afraid.

Choose and write one of the promises discussed above that you think you can lean into today.

____

____

____

____

____

____

From Linda's Journey

March 3, 2000

4:00 a.m.

We are told that Ron's condition is grave.

When the extensive surgery is finally over and we can see him in the recovery room for a few minutes, my minister grips my arm. He says to me, "This won't be pretty. He won't look like himself. Can you do this?"

I nod, but nothing has prepared me for the still and gray figure on the stretcher or the tubes and monitors everywhere. I touch Ron on a bare spot near his right shoulder.

"Ron," I whisper. "I love you."

His eyes fly open, and for one second before they close again, he smiles.

It is the same smile I remember from our wedding day.

That smile reminds me that God still holds Ron in the shadow of his care.

Take a Moment

What comfort have you received from Psalm 91:1? Read the verse prayerfully and write your responses to the questions that follow.

Whoever dwells in the shelter of the Most High will rest in the shadow of the Almighty (Psalm 91:1)

1. What have you learned about God's shadow in this chapter?

____

____

____

____

2. Where is one physical place you can find rest right now?

____

____

____

____

Prayer for Shelter

Lord, I come to you weary from the weight of caring for someone I love. The days are long, and the burdens are heavy. Thank you for inviting me to dwell with you, safe in the shelter of your shadow. Remind me that I don't have to carry the weight of caregiving alone. You are covering me with your constant care. Teach me to rest in your promises and find peace in your presence. I know that you will walk this road with me and keep me in your shadow. In Jesus' name, amen.

CHAPTER 2

Building Trust While in Refuge

Verse for the Journey: I will say of the Lord, "He is my refuge and my fortress, my God, in whom I trust." (Psalm 91:2)

From Linda's Journey

March 3, 2000

5:00 a.m.

The phone next to the bed jangles loudly, and I reach across the sleeping bodies of my daughter and my son. They went to their respective rooms two hours ago, but eventually dragged their pillows and blankets down the hall and crawled into bed with me. I grab the phone quickly, my heart pounding. Is it the hospital?

"Hello?"

The voice on the other end is faint and choked with tears. “Is he still alive?”

Recognizing the voice of my oldest son, in New Orleans during a college break, I shake my head to clear the cobwebs of sleep deprivation.

It feels like a lifetime ago when I left a message for Dennis on an answering machine. While family and friends have supported me on this awful night, Dennis has had only the cold comfort of a terse “Dennis, Dad’s been in an accident. It’s bad. Call me when you get this message.”

“Is he still alive?” my son repeats, almost screaming now.

I find my voice. “Yes. Yes, hon, he’s alive. He’s in intensive care and he’s had several surgeries and it’s critical, but he’s alive.”

“What happened?”

“An accident,” I say. “He was coming home from work when a pickup truck ran a red light and hit the driver’s side of Dad’s car. That’s really all I know.”

I run through the litany of damage to organs I could not have named yesterday: spleen, pancreas, aorta, diaphragm, liver, trachea. I shudder to myself at the extent of injury a human being can sustain and still live.

“But he’ll be alright?” Dennis asks.

"We don't know yet. There's a lot that can go wrong. But when I left the hospital last night—well, earlier this morning—he was stable. I'll call in a few hours."

"I'm coming home now. Bill says he'll drive me. I should be there to help you."

I shake my head. "No. Not yet. Get some rest first. There's nothing you can do here. Just pray for Dad. For all of us."

Remembering a comment Allen made to me last night, I smile. "Allen says he'll lock the doors and protect us. He wants us to feel safe without Dad in the house."

Dennis gives a small laugh. "I'm sure Allen will do his best." My son sighs. "Okay. I'll call you later. But I'm still coming home tomorrow. New Orleans is fun, but I need to be with my family."

We say our goodbyes and hang up. I glance from the phone to the bed. Following the order of my husband's surgeon, the kids and I will call off unnecessary activity for today. I tuck the covers around my sleeping children and whisper a prayer.

Dear God, I need to trust my husband to you right now. I have no idea what will happen, no idea what today may bring. I want to trust you completely, but I'm not there yet. Help me.

Patting the blankets over Bonnie and Allen, I wonder if maybe this is where trust begins, in the quiet and in the whispers. I will need, I realize, a safe place to lean my soul when I grow weary.

I will need a refuge.

Rest in God's Protection

I don't know what is happening with your loved one right now, but I know this: staying in the presence of God will bring you the peace you will need for this journey. The activity surrounding illness will pull you in many directions, and there may be tough decisions to make. No matter what the trouble, God is our refuge. Peter referred to him as our light in a dark place.

We also have the prophetic message as something completely reliable, and you will do well to pay attention to it, as to a light shining in a dark place, until the day dawns and the morning star rises in your hearts. (2 Peter 1:19)

Note the words "completely reliable" in the NIV translation. Even when our way is dark, we have the light of God. Always and forever, we can rely on him. We can trust in his refuge. But trust does not always come easily. I had a lot to learn about trust in the months following Ron's car accident.

Several key words from Psalm 91:2 in the NIV translation helped me grow my trust. If you have a pen handy, try to write your own definitions of the words without looking them up.

Say____________________________________

Refuge__________________________________

Fortress_________________________________

Trust___________________________________

The word *say* can be translated as "declare." Declarative sentences are bold and confident, stating the truth with conviction. The speaker of Psalm 91 is boldly declaring that God is bigger than any problem we might face. *Refuge* refers to a place where one retreats when circumstances are hard or there is danger. It has the connotation of "shelter from the rain." *Fortress* similarly refers to a place of safety, but a fortress is designed for battle. Whoever or whatever is attacking, God, your stronghold, will keep you safe. Because God has always proven himself to be *trustworthy* and to keep his promises, we know that God is in control.

Write down one trouble you feel ready to trust to God today.

____

____

____

____

____

Renew Through God's Word

While Ron was in the ICU, my trust in God deepened. That did not happen all at once but came gradually, as I witnessed how God provided experienced medical personnel to care for Ron and as members of our church provided for our physical needs. Ron required many surgeries to repair the damage done to his body. I had to place complete trust in both God and the surgeons.

My children and I did our best to make Ron's hospital room a place of refuge where Ron could recover between surgeries. I hung cards and posters saying "Get Well" from my middle school students.

The room was also a fortress where we discussed the medical team's plans for draining Ron's lungs and repairing his aorta. Our minister and church family showed up with hymns and prayers, filling that sterile space with reminders of God's presence. Their voices softened the hard edges of suffering.

An understanding of God as refuge became more real to me day by caregiving day. Considering a few of the many people in the Bible who sought God as both refuge and fortress can strengthen that understanding.

The Young Convert's Choice

In the book of Ruth, a young Moabite woman makes a life-changing decision. After the death of her husband, Ruth chooses not to return to her own family or gods and instead stays with her Israelite mother-in-law, Naomi. At Ruth 1:16, Ruth embraces the God of Israel and commits to an unknown future with trust and courage.

But Ruth replied, *"Don't urge me to leave you or to turn back from you. Where you go I will go, and where you stay I will stay. Your people will be my people and your God my God."*

Ruth's decision brought her not just to a new home but to a new refuge, as she learned to trust the God of Naomi. You may find yourself stepping into a new and uncertain season as you walk beside your loved one through illness. As Ron's needs changed, for example, I had to learn to change his feeding tube and care for his pic lines. Each day brought a new challenge.

Like Ruth's journey, caregiving requires trust, sacrifice, and courage. And like Ruth, you are invited to take refuge under God's care—not just for your loved one, but for yourself. God offers his refuge not only as a place to hide but as a place to belong.

Write down one new responsibility or concern you've had to take on in this season of your life.

A Disciple's Doubt

The disciple Thomas is often remembered for his doubt. When the other disciples told him that Jesus had risen, he struggled to believe. He didn't trust their words; he wanted proof. Thomas honestly expressed his doubt.

> *So the other disciples told him, "We have seen the Lord!" But he said to them, "Unless I see the nail marks in his hands and put my finger where the nails were, and put my hand into his side, I will not believe." (John 20:25)*

A week later, Jesus appeared again and met Thomas and his doubt. With compassion, Jesus invited Thomas to do precisely what he had asked—to see, to touch, to believe.

Thomas' story reminds us that doubt doesn't disqualify us from God's love or his promises. Jesus didn't reject Thomas for doubting. Instead, he met him with compassion and gently led him toward trust. Trust grows when we bring our honest questions to Jesus and let him meet us there. At the beginning of my caregiving journey, I doubted that our financial needs could be met, that I could be strong enough, and that our family would adjust. God showed me that he could provide in all ways.

Write down what you are doubting today and what you think would help you trust God more fully.

____

____

____

____

____

A Call for Strength

Sometimes words fail us. In moments of deep grief, pain, or exhaustion, we may not even know what to pray. Caregivers often live in that space where they are uncertain, weary, and wondering what the next day will bring. Even Jesus experienced this kind of anguish.

As he hung on the cross, he gave voice to that deep human ache. We read his words in Matthew 27:46.

About three in the afternoon, Jesus cried out in a loud voice, "Eli, Eli, lema sabachthani?" (which means "My God, my God, why have you forsaken me?")

In that cry, we hear both the depth of suffering and the depth of trust. Even in agony, Jesus called on the name of God. He didn't hide his pain but brought it straight to the Father.

When you don't have the strength for long prayers, simply saying "My God" can be enough. Saying those two words is not a sign of weakness but a powerful declaration of trust, even when everything else feels uncertain. I said it many times during Ron's surgeries when I had no words left to pray.

Write "My God" here as many times as you need. Let it be your prayer today.

____

____

____

____

____

Remember God's Faithfulness

I know caregiving may be a scary place for you. I do not know how long you might be there, but you can always find refuge in God, even if you are visiting the ICU or sitting in a waiting room. God is completely dependable. Remember what God has already done. He has no record of failure. We can rely on him wholly, like on a best friend. You can always trust God.

After Ron was injured, my best friend, Chris, came to the hospital that night to comfort and support me. I had called the church to start a prayer chain, and Chris called my cell phone. I told her not to come, but she came anyway because best friends are like that. They always come.

God's Word shows us this again and again. Think of Joseph, betrayed by his brothers, falsely accused, thrown in prison, forgotten by men, but never forgotten by God. Through every betrayal and disappointment, God continued to walk with Joseph. At Genesis 50:20, we read Joseph's understanding of what God had been doing in his life.

You intended to harm me, but God intended it for good to accomplish what is now being done, the saving of many lives.

The same God who formed the stars is sitting next to you right now. He is your truest friend, offering you comfort, strength, and steady love. His friendship can feel like a warm hug from a favorite aunt, the tight embrace of a child, or the compassionate arms of a good friend.

Write a brief description of what having God's friendship feels like to you.

From Linda's Journey

March 3, 2000

9:00 a.m.

Bonnie and I enter the cubicle on tiptoe, hesitant to disturb the silence of the ICU. Ron lies on a raised bed, his arms still bound by tubes and straps. The ventilator makes his chest rise and fall, its steady whoosh filling the room with mechanical breath. I touch his hand, and he stirs. On the other side of the bed, Bonnie rests her hand on her father's shoulder. He shudders, like a man caught in a bad dream, and slowly opens his eyes.

We hold our breath, waiting.

Then we see it, that spark of recognition. His lopsided smile breaks through, and our tears fall onto the bedsheets. I want to speak—so much—but words don't matter right now. Only presence matters. Minutes—or hours—pass like this. Nurses with crepe-soled shoes come and go, checking vital signs glowing green on the monitor overhead. The world outside fades. For now, this place, this fragile moment, is where we stay.

God is our refuge. Not the machines, not the monitors, not even the capable nurses. But God. Right here in this room.

Suddenly, Ron jerks. His eyes fly open, and his hands flail.

"He wants to tell you something," says a nurse, pulling a pad of paper and pencil from her pocket.

She positions the pencil in Ron's hand and holds the pad steady.

Bonnie and I watch as Ron spells out his first words after the accident.

God saved my life.

The battle ahead will be long, but we know we are not alone. God has carried us this far. He will not stop now. He will continue to be our refuge and our fortress.

I dig a little deeper into my trust of God.

If you could, what would you like to say to your loved one right now? Write it here, then say it if you are able, even if the words will not be heard.

____

____

____

____

____

Take a Moment

Psalm 91:2 reminds us that God invites us to declare him as our safe place. Pray over the verse for a few minutes, then write your responses to the questions that follow. Remember that prayer is a safe place to talk with God, who will always be your refuge.

> *I will say of the Lord, "He is my refuge and my fortress, my God, in whom I trust." (Psalm 91:2)*

1. Where do you usually turn when life feels overwhelming, when fear creeps in, when exhaustion pulls you under, or when answers don't come?

2. Where are you struggling to trust God right now?

3. What would it look like to rest in God as your refuge, even if you don't yet have all the answers your caregiving situation requires?

Prayer for Building Trust

Lord, you remain my refuge and my fortress. In the middle of fear, confusion, and exhaustion, I declare you are trustworthy. Help me to recognize the small blessings that surround me and to rest in the safety of your love. When I have no words, remind me I can always call out to you, my God. Build my trust that no matter where I am, you are near. Enable me to trust you in every circumstance. In Jesus' name, amen.

CHAPTER 3

Remaining Safe in God's Care

Verse for the Journey: Surely he will save you from the fowler's snare and the deadly pestilence. (Psalm 91:3)

From Linda's Journey

March 6, 2000
9:00 p.m.

When I get home from the last hospital visit of the day, I spend the evening returning phone calls to those whose numbers the kids have added to the notepad by the phone. I try to keep the conversations brief, since I've worked a full day and been to the hospital twice. But I am often asked questions I cannot immediately answer.

"Do you need anything?"

"Is there anything we can do?"

"What is Ron's prognosis?"

During calls like these, most people concentrate on Ron: his vital signs, his spirits, his next surgery. There is always a next surgery. Once in a great while, someone will ask how I am managing this. My response is always the same.

"God is taking care of me."

Some days, I feel God's arms around me. Other days, when Ron's condition is precarious, I struggle to feel anything but worry.

The kids have gone to bed by the time I finish the phone calls and prepare my schoolbag for my next day of teaching. Before tumbling into my lonely bed, I wander up the steps and first check on my two sleeping offspring.

Bonnie snuggles with the crocheted pig her grandmother made long ago. Her room is strewn with discarded clothing and movie posters. She looks like a typical teenager, but she has needed a maturity beyond most of her peers. Right now, she is her brother Allen's substitute mother.

Allen's room is filled with Star Wars posters and well-worn action figures. His lanky frame barely fits beneath his R2-D2 quilt. One long leg has slipped out from under the covers. I gently lift it back onto the mattress and tuck the quilt around him. As I step back, my foot bumps something hard beneath the bed. Curious, I crouch down and pull out a hammer, one I recognize from Ron's toolbox.

I smile and balance the hammer in my hand. Like Luke Skywalker defending Princess Leia, Allen is keeping his promise to protect Bonnie and me, storing a hammer nearby in case he needs to save us in the night. I stow the hammer under the bed, strangely comforted by the care of a fourteen-year-old boy, then step into the hallway.

I breathe deeply. God doesn't need a hammer to defend us. His weapons are much greater. His care is not limited to churches or hospitals.

He meets me where I am.

Lord, keep my children safe in your care, I pray. Help me to rely fully on you.

Rest in God's Protection

For a caregiver, remaining safe in God's care does not always mean finding physical protection or escape from hardship. The longer Ron's hospitalization lasted, the more I needed to lean on God for a deep, inner assurance. Eventually, I realized that God's care of me was very specific to each situation I faced.

It helped me to know that God saw me wherever I was, whether at home or in Ron's hospital room, a waiting room, a cafeteria, or a classroom. I was not alone in this exhausting journey. Though my world had spun out of control, God was still holding my heart and mind in his hands, helping me understand that while my husband's care was very important to me, it was even more important to God.

Seeking to remain safe in God's care was not just for physical protection as I drove from home to school to hospital and home again. Trying to absorb medical information and make quick decisions left me mentally drained and vulnerable as well. Psalm 121:7-8 renewed me.

The Lord will keep you from all harm—he will watch over your life; the Lord will watch over your coming and going both now and forevermore.

Like a caring parent or friend, God continually watches over us, concerned about every aspect of our lives. He is aware of our struggles and is always present with us. He moves with us from the hospital to our homes, from school to the store, from the bathroom to the bedside. Even late at night, when my children had gone to bed and I was left with a long list of phone messages to return, I realized God had not retired for the night but was at my side through every call.

What type of care do you need from God now: physical, emotional, or spiritual? Prayerfully seek that type of care from God as you put your most significant current need into words here.

Renew Through God's Word

Comparing biblical translations can often renew our understanding. In the King James Bible, Psalm 91:3 states, "Surely he shall deliver you from the snare of the fowler and from the perilous pestilence."

Deliver is a strong English word with two uses in Old Testament translations. The first usage, translating the Hebrew word natan, means "to turn over to another or rescue." The second usage, translating the Hebrew word nasal, means "to draw out or snatch away." Consider the impressive image of God's hand reaching in and rescuing you from danger, fear, despair, and weariness.

The word translated "snare" in Psalm 91:3 has both literal and metaphorical meanings in the Bible. In Psalm 91, it is being used to refer to both a cord that tied with a slipknot to catch a bird's legs (Amos 3:5) and an ambush manufactured by the devil.

A fowler is someone who hunts and traps birds, but Bible translations also use the word *fowler* in reference to Satan and traps he designs to cause doubt about God's care of us. Psalm 124:7 assures us we can escape from such a trap as a bird might slip out of a snare.

We have escaped like a bird from the fowler's snare; the snare has been broken and we have escaped.

On the caregiving journey, we can trust God to keep us from being trapped by circumstances and by our emotional responses to them.

Imagine God snatching a bird from the trap of a fowler. Here, draw or write a brief description of that moment. Note what it feels like to be the bird God rescues.

____

____

____

____

____

Doubt is difficult to avoid when a situation is dire and we don't know what will happen next. Rather than dwelling on the doubts in your mind at such times, try to focus on trusting that God is with you and caring for you. While waiting out a long surgery, I would read in my Bible or knit, trying to keep doubt and worry from my mind. Doubt often came knocking, but I refused to give it my attention.

John warns us to consider what we give our attention.

> *For everything in the world—the lust of the flesh, the lust of the eyes, and the pride of life—comes not from the Father but from the world. (1 John 2:16)*

Keeping your mind set on God requires vigilance, especially when you are weary and many burdens weigh on your shoulders.

When doubt or fear tries to trap you, what helps you refocus your heart on God's care? Write down one way you might remind yourself, as needed, that God's hand is always ready to rescue you.

____

____

____

____

____

Remember God's Faithfulness

I'm sure you're wondering about the future—about how your loved one's illness will change your life and the lives of your family. You may be concerned about the loss of a paycheck and, if you have children in the house, losing another adult authority figure. I get it. I had those practical concerns as well.

Just for now, allow yourself not to worry about them. Get a cup of coffee, tea, or soda and take five minutes to remember.

Remember what God has already done. Hebrews 13:8 says, "Jesus is the same yesterday and today and forever." Whatever God has done for you in the past, he will continue to do in the future.

I worried about how we were going to make the mortgage when Ron could not work. In the first month, my husband's coworkers started a collection that resulted in the exact amount I needed. For the second month, someone from our church made an anonymous donation. There was never a month God did not provide. I'll admit I was often on edge the day before the mortgage was due, but we never missed a payment. Remembering God's previous care helped me to put my energies into other issues, knowing God would provide the needed funds.

List one need you will ask—with confidence—for God to provide.

____

____

____

____

____

From Linda's Journey

April 10, 2000

6:00 p.m.

I am alone in my husband's hospital room. Ron was heavily sedated when I saw him at 1:45, just before they wheeled him into surgery for his collapsed lung. He will not be returning to this floor after the procedure, so I busy myself packing up his meager belongings: cards, socks, shaving gear, underwear, a few sports magazines. I take down the cards from my school students, a colorful array of sixth-grade drawings.

Ron will go to the surgical wing when he is out of recovery. The patient's bag the nurses gave me is usually used to transport belongings home, but this one will rest in the trunk of my car for a few days. I give the place where we have made Ron's home for the last five weeks one more look. His Bible lies open on the windowsill. I suppose our minister must have left it there when he visited earlier.

I pick up the Bible. It is open to the book of John, and there, underlined in a shaky hand, is Ron's favorite Bible verse, John 3:16: "For God so loved the world that he gave his one and only son, that whoever believes in him shall not perish but have everlasting life."

Underneath the verse, my husband has written "I'm a whoever."

Tears prick my eyes as I trace Ron's words with my fingertip. That simple sentence isn't just a note but a declaration. Ron knows he belongs to God.

I take the plastic bag out to my car and return to the waiting room outside the operating theater, Ron's Bible in my hands.

Write out a Bible verse favored by your loved one or by you. If you do not have a favorite verse, please use my husband's.

____

____

____

____

____

Take a Moment

Psalm 91:3 tells us that we can remain safe in God's care no matter where we are. Take a moment to reread the verse and write your responses to the questions that follow.

> *Surely he will save you from the fowler's snare and the deadly pestilence. (Psalm 91:3)*

1. In what areas of your life do you sense God's protective care most strongly? Are there situations where you may have missed seeing his hand of safety?

2. How does knowing that God's care is constant and unchanging bring you comfort, especially during times of uncertainty or fear?

3. What steps can you take today to reaffirm your trust in God's protection, both in everyday life and during more difficult moments?

Prayer for Safety

Lord, thank you for seeing traps I cannot see and for snatching me from snares meant to hold me down. Protect my heart from fear, my mind from doubt, and my soul from discouragement. Remind me, moment by moment, that I and my loved one remain in your care. You keep us safe, no matter where we are, because you are always beside us. In Jesus' name, amen.

CHAPTER 4

Receiving the Cover of God's Faithfulness

Verse for the Journey: He will cover you with his feathers, and under his wings you will find refuge; his faithfulness will be your shield and rampart. (Psalm 91:4)

From Linda's Journey

April 12, 2000
4:00 p.m.

Wild violets have grown up in the backyard. I discover the tiny purple stars against the green crabgrass as Allen and I rake. I marvel that any flowers survived the harsh winter of snow, ice, and neglect. Yet here they are, struggling to push themselves out of the cold earth toward the pale spring sunshine. Despite last summer's drought and the subzero temperatures of the winter, these small flowers have survived and grace our backyard with their beauty.

And somehow, by God's grace, my family has survived too.

Ron's ongoing hospitalizations have thrown obstacles in our path that we never expected. Long and complicated surgeries and infections. Mounting medical bills. A leaky water heater. Car repairs. We have struggled to survive, pushing our heads above our circumstances and stretching toward the sun.

I pause in my raking, enjoying the beauty of these tiny wild flowers. Somewhere above, a bird calls from a branch of the maple tree, hidden but near. It reminds me that God's care is just as near, his wings already extended to cover my family. The book of Matthew tells us, "And why do you worry about clothes? See how the flowers of the field grow. They do not labor or spin. Yet I tell you that not even Solomon in all his splendor was dressed like one of these" (6:28–29, NIV). I consider these small flowers a gift from God, a reminder of the cycle of the seasons and the new birth of spring. In the dark, dankness of tragedy and despair, the children and I have continued to feel the love of God.

We are secure. We are safe. Our spirits are warmed by the sun. We do not yet know if Ron will fully recover or when he might come home. The predicted four weeks have now stretched into a new month and a new season.

The phone has stopped its constant ringing. I send a group email each afternoon to update our church members, friends, and family on Ron's condition. Doing so allows me time in the evening with the kids. We are in a calm period now, with no surgeries in the last two days.

It may not last.

But what will last is God's ability to shelter us. Like a protective parent bird covering its young, he wraps his wings around us.

His faithfulness keeps us safe.

Rest in God's Protection

Take a few moments to rest in the refuge God offers. While we are as foolish and as weak as little birds, God will keep each of us safe beneath his wings. His promises are individual to every person.

Imagine receiving the cover of God's faithfulness for you specifically. In what ways is God spreading his wings over you? He may be giving you the strength to help your spouse wash and change, patience when you have to explain the same medical procedure for the third time to your spouse or relatives, or comfort when you sit beside a hospital bed waiting for answers.

God's wings will surround you when you feel invisible and uphold you when you're too exhausted to pray. God is a shelter to us at all times, no matter where we are.

Imagine what being under the wings of God might feel like to your senses. Write your impressions here.

____

____

____

____

____

We are often unaware of the dangers from which God shields us—dangers seen and unseen, natural and spiritual. Psalm 31:20 reminds us of God's protective shelter.

In the shelter of your presence, you hide them from all human intrigues: you keep them safe in your dwelling from accusing tongues.

What is God sheltering you from at this moment? Are there harsh words or judgments about your caregiving decisions? Does self-doubt whisper in your ear? The many medical procedures my husband needed were unfamiliar to me, with names that sounded frightening. In the midst of my self-doubt, I learned to pause, breathe, and seek shelter under God's wings before signing the permission form.

As mentioned in chapter 1, Psalm 27:5 assures us that God is with us in a troubled day.

For in the day of trouble he will keep me safe in his dwelling; he will hide me in the shelter of his sacred tent and set me high upon a rock.

Consider again the image of the rock from Isaiah 32:2, also mentioned in chapter 1.

Each one will be like a shelter from the wind and a refuge from the storm, like streams of water in the desert and the shadow of a great rock in a thirsty land.

In these verses, God's protection is described as a safe dwelling, a sacred tent, a quiet shelter, a dry refuge, a refreshing stream, a cooling shadow.

Using one of the images of God's protection from the preceding verses, write down one way the Lord is keeping you safe at this time.

Not only can you shelter under the protection of God's wings, but God will reward your faithfulness to your spouse, as he did the faithfulness of Ruth toward her mother-in-law Naomi.

May the Lord repay you for what you have done. May you be richly rewarded by the Lord, the God of Israel, under whose wings you have come to take refuge. (Ruth 2:12)

Write down a few possible rewards for caregiving that would be particularly meaningful to you.

____

____

____

____

____

Renew Through God's Word

Look back at the verses quoted in the last section and notice the repetition of the theme of a shelter or refuge. Scripture repeatedly shows God's protective nature. Not only does he protect us from those who would harm us, but he provides us with tools we can use to face the enemies of caregiving. God equips us with faith as our shield and hope as our sword.

To gain further understanding of God's ability to equip us, compare the King James translation of Psalm 91:4 to the New International Version.

He will cover you with his feathers, and under his wings you will find refuge; his faithfulness will be your shield and rampart. (New International Version)

He shall cover thee with his feathers, and under his wings shalt thou trust; his truth shall be thy shield and buckler. (King James Version)

Each version uses different words to express the same sense of protection God offers to us. The King James Bible uses the words *shield* and *buckler*, while the New International Version uses *shield* and *rampart*. No matter what the protection is called, God's faithfulness surrounds us completely. In Bible times, two types of shields served as protective armament. You've probably seen both kinds in movies. The shield was round and held close to the body by one arm in hand-to-hand combat. The buckler was a long, rectangular shield that covered the entire body of the soldier as an army advanced on an enemy. Whether we are in hand-to-hand combat with one enemy or surrounded by an army of enemies, God is protecting us with his shield and buckler.

If you have ever visited a fort, you might have seen or even climbed onto a rampart, a protective barrier or a wall surrounding the top of a fortress or fort. A rampart is another image of how closely God protects us and how he desires to keep us secure and safe.

Draw or write a description of a rampart, shield, or buckler protecting you.

____

____

____

____

____

Doubts, fears, and exhaustion can be enemies of a caregiver. We have the power to ward off their attacks because God's faithfulness is our armor. We can take refuge in him, hide behind his ramparts, and use his armaments for protection.

Remember God's Faithfulness

I don't know how long your loved one has been ill or injured, and I don't know how long this difficult season will last for you. I do know that God's promises are based not on current circumstances but on the very character of God, who longs to gather you to him.

If you find it very difficult to set aside your worries, I understand. I'm the same way. It seems I can trust God for five minutes, then I'm back to worrying. So, I learned to trust God with my worries five minutes at a time.

Try trusting God with your worries for five minutes. Set a timer if you like. For the next five minutes, choose to believe all the promises from God explored in this chapter.

God will spread his wings over you.

He will shelter you in his wings.

He will calm your doubts and uncertainty.

He will be your protector, your shield.

As part of your five minutes, be willing to be gathered under God's wings as you reflect on the following quotations by people who experienced the fulfillment of God's promises.

> *"Let God's promises shine on your problems."*
> —Corrie ten Boom, *The Hiding Place,* 1971

> *"God never calls His people to accomplish anything without promising to supply their every need."*
> —Charles R. Swindoll, *Jesus: The Greatest Life of All,* 2009

> *"Every promise of Scripture is a writing of God, which may be pleaded before Him with this reasonable request, 'Do as Thou hast said.' The Heavenly Father will not break His Word to His own child."*
> —Charles H. Spurgeon, "*The Plea of Faith*", 1856

Psalm 91:4 is an anchor for these promises. God offers gentle shelter and unshakeable reliability.

Write out one of the promises from God just mentioned that you can now claim as your own.

____

____

____

____

____

From Linda's Journey

April 23, 2000

Palm Sunday

7:00 a.m.

It is a rainy day with a faint rumble of thunder in the distance, and my tears add to the melancholy of the day. It has been forty-five days since Ron's car accident, forty-five days that I have spent trying to hold the world together on my own.

I am beyond exhausted, yet my mind cannot sleep. I wake at odd moments in the night and stare at the luminescent numbers on the alarm clock at my bedside. Will this nightmare ever end?

Earlier, I paced the halls of the hospital and wondered if I was to blame for any delay in Ron's recovery. After a brief stay at a rehabilitation center, Ron is back in the hospital because of pneumonia. Should I have taken him home instead of sending him to a place with daily nursing? Would it have made a difference?

My friends tell me Ron's pneumonia is not my fault. My father-in-law tells me it is.

I climb out of bed now and stare out the window, tracing a raindrop down the glass pane. Despite the rain, birds are chirping the arrival of spring and Eastertide. Perhaps the birds know something we often forget. Does their innate faith in the Father trust that sunshine will follow rain?

Palm Sunday recalls Jesus' triumphant ride into Jerusalem, a ride soon followed by betrayal and crucifixion. Then the sun rose on Easter Sunday, and so did our Lord! Similarly, Ron's injuries have battered his body, but his soul remains intact.

I listen to the birds and take refuge in God.

Take another five minutes and imagine yourself continuing to take refuge under the shelter of God's wings. Consider that your loved one is also discouraged. Imagine God speaking tenderly to your loved one. Write down words of comfort and strength God might whisper to draw your loved one under his wings.

____

____

____

____

Take a Moment

Psalm 91:4 assures us that God is our refuge. Read the verse again and write your responses to the questions that follow.

He will cover you with his feathers, and under his wings you will find refuge; his faithfulness will be your shield and rampart. (Psalm 91:4)

1. In your caregiving journey, where have you most clearly seen or felt God's protection and comfort?

2. What practical steps can you take each day to remind yourself that God's shelter is available—especially during moments of exhaustion or doubt?

3. How might trusting God's faithful care help you find the strength and peace needed to continue giving care to your loved one?

Prayer for Coverage

Dear Lord, when I am too tired to move, too uncertain to decide, and too discouraged to hope, hide me under your wings. Be my quiet place, my shield in battle, my shelter from the storm. Let your faithfulness surround me like a fortress and whisper truth to every lie I hear. Remind me that I am never alone. Not in the hospital, my home, or my season of waiting. Thank you for seeing me, covering me, and caring for me and my loved one. In Jesus' name, amen.

CHAPTER 5

Braving the Night

Verses for the Journey: You will not fear the terror of the night, nor the arrow that flies by day, nor the pestilence that stalks in the darkness, nor the plague that destroys at midday. (Psalm 91:5–6)

From Linda's Journey

April 24, 2000
10:00 p.m.

I sleep on Ron's side of the bed most nights. It sags slightly from the weight of his absence, and I curl myself into the hollow, seeking the familiar. Mine has been a slow trek across the expanse of my queen-sized mattress.

I began, in those first horrible nights after the accident, on my accustomed side of the bed, the latest words from Dr. Huffman, my husband's surgeon, replaying in my mind. Another surgery. An unknown infection. A return to the ICU. The silence in my room was heavy. No sounds of sonorous breathing punctuated the night; no heavy leg flung over mine pressed me into the mattress; no warm presence wrestled with the sheets or pulled the blanket from my shoulders.

My nights were quiet. Empty. Fearful.

Slowly, across many nights, I inched my way into the bed's middle, drawn toward the far side by a pillow still holding the faint fragrance of Ron's aftershave.

The middle was awful. I felt like the spine of a book with two wide blank pages on either side of me, solitary in a great expanse of unfilled space where once there had hardly been enough room for two. I continued my progression toward the other side, crawling across the cold sheets, seeking comfort and warmth.

I sleep on Ron's side now, inhaling his lingering male scent, wrapping my own arms around my waist, and waiting out the long hours until morning. There are nights I sleep soundly, dreaming of Ron, then awaken suddenly, startled to find myself facing the room from a different angle.

My life has changed. My point of view has changed. God is calming my fears, one at a time, and teaching me to release them into his care.

Rest in God's Protection

How are you sleeping, my friend? Nights can be especially difficult for the caregiver suddenly alone. During the first two weeks of Ron's hospitalization, Bonnie and Allen usually joined me in my bedroom. When they eventually returned to their own rooms, I felt the pain of loneliness. While fears remained, I learned to give them to God one at a time.

The good news is that God will always protect you, day or night. While we may not escape all dangers—your loved one's illness or injury proves that—God will protect us from all evil and the fear of evil. As Psalm 91 tells us, God is our refuge. We need not be stuck deep in fear. Take heart in these words from Isaiah 26:3:

You will keep in perfect peace those whose minds are steadfast, because they trust in you.

Perfect peace is a condition that keeps our souls free from the burden of worry, as if a weight has been lifted from our shoulders. The Hebrew word for peace is *shalom* and carries with it the beautiful idea of wholeness and health. Isaiah wrote his verse about perfect peace during a dark time in Israel's history and reminds us that peace is not dependent on our surroundings but on God's faithful presence.

Write how you would define perfect peace in your life right now.

God wants peace, not fear, to be our portion. Peace is one of the nine gifts of the Holy Spirit (Galatians 5:22–23). In the weeks following my husband's car accident, I was often afraid of what the future might hold. Each day seemed to bring another problem, medical or financial. I frequently read Philippians 4:6–7, which became my life verses.

> *Do not be anxious about anything, but in every situation, by prayer and petition, with thanksgiving, present your requests to God. And the peace of God, which transcends all understanding, will guard your hearts and your minds in Christ Jesus.*

Just as I slowly shifted my position to Ron's side of the bed, I slowly came to accept the gift of peace in my mind and heart.

God's love for us drives out any fear and gives us power. From the assurances found in Ephesians 3:16–18, we can trust that the love of Christ is wider than any space in a bed or heart.

I pray that out of his glorious riches he may strengthen you with power through his Spirit in your inner being, so that Christ may dwell in your hearts through faith. And I pray that you, being rooted and established in love, may have power, together with all the Lord's holy people, to grasp how wide and long and high and deep is the love of Christ.

We are rooted in the love of Christ. God's love is so wide and so deep, so high and so long, that no matter what size bed you are sleeping in now, God can fill it. You will not be alone. When the phone rings at midnight with an emergency call from the doctor, when regret over past decisions tries to take hold or anxiety about the unknown races through your mind, picture God guarding you, pushing your terrors away.

Write a few words about how the reality of God's protective love and the image of God guarding you make you feel.

____

____

____

____

____

Renew Through God's Word

Psalm 91:5–6 mentions several threats that can fill us with fear. These threats—whether human, physical, or emotional—occur at any time of the day, but in the ancient world, darkness was a vulnerable time. There were no electric lights to brighten the night, and attacks from wild animals or bandits were feared.

Caregivers experience their own versions of these "terrors," including emotional pain, financial pressure, sleepless nights, medical decisions, and loneliness. Take a moment to reflect on the questions that follow:

- What "terrors of the night" have you faced lately? Calls from the hospital? Loneliness?
- What unexpected "arrows" have come your way? High medical bills? Unknown test results?
- Is there an anxiety, regret, or upcoming medical procedure "stalking" your thoughts in this season?
- What kind of "plague" seems to be draining your energy or peace?

There are a lot of things we might fear, especially in the darkness. And if you are sitting alone in the hospital at night, it can be a very scary place. Whatever nighttime alarms or daytime worries we face, we can draw encouragement from the description of the Holy

Spirit at 1 John 4:4, where John speaks of overcoming false prophets.

> *You, dear children, are from God and have overcome them, because the one who is in you is greater than the one who is in the world.*

You don't have to face terrors alone. Darkness or light, night or day, God's Spirit is always there to protect you. His love surrounds you with twenty-four-hour protection. The two verses that follow are among many that assure us of God's faithful protection. Underline words that refer to fear. Circle words proclaiming what God gives us.

> *Don't be afraid, little flock, for your Father has been pleased to give you the kingdom. (Luke 12:32)*

> *He said to his disciples, "Why are you so afraid? Do you still have no faith?"(Mark 4:40)*

Despite the truth of these proclamations, we continue in fear when we try to take care of problems on our own. You may try to plan and scheme how you can work your caregiving challenges out in your own strength. I know I tried! But ultimately, we can't do life by ourselves. We can only do it with God's help.

What fears are you carrying right now? As you write them here, commit each fear to God. He will surely answer your commitment with his protection.

Remember God's Faithfulness

You and your loved one made promises to one another at marriage, a covenant to love and care for each other. Regardless of whether you wrote your own vows or used traditional ones, you likely promised to support each other no matter what. And now you are in the middle of "no matter what." In caregiving, staying faithful to your commitment to your spouse is often a challenge.

God is and will remain a witness to the vows of your marriage (Malachi 2:14). Throughout Scripture, God has made his own covenants with people. The Old Testament covenants are the Noahic covenant (Genesis 8:20–9:17), the Abrahamic covenant (Genesis 17:9–14), the Mosaic covenant (Exodus

31:12–18), and the Davidic covenant (2 Samuel 7). In the New Testament, we read of an even better covenant Jesus guaranteed for us.

> *And it was not without an oath! Others became priests without any oath, but he became a priest with an oath when God said to him: "The Lord has sworn and will not change his mind: 'You are a priest forever.'" Because of this oath, Jesus has become the guarantor of a better covenant. (Hebrews 7:20–22)*

Not only has Jesus guaranteed for us a better covenant, but he has given us the Holy Spirit to comfort and to guide us (Acts 2:38). Reflect on what this covenant and gift really mean for you at this moment in your life when "no matter what" has happened. Even when others don't understand the caregiving path you have chosen, God sees the promises you have kept.

Write here a promise you have kept on your caregiving journey. Then imagine God's pleasure in your commitment.

My role as caregiver to my husband began not with his car accident in March 2000 but in 1996, when mental issues started to plague him. Realizing the financial support of my family now fell on me, I responded within our marriage covenant and took a teaching position at a school that offered an increased salary. Deciding to remain with Ron during the years of his illnesses was difficult, but I knew God would stand beside me.

Caregiving requires courage you didn't know you had. But God knew you would need that courage, and he promises to shelter you and to be your refuge when you face tough choices.

If you were to renew your vows to your loved one, would you change them? Might this event of "no matter what" in your lives make your marriage promise to your spouse even stronger? Write a new vow to your loved one.

____

____

____

____

____

From Linda's Journey

July 10, 1999

10:30 a.m.

I go to our minister before resigning from the Christian school where I had taught for three years, a list of pros and cons trembling in my hand. The offer from the public school is almost three times my academy salary.

"Your choice seems simple," my pastor says. "Your first obligation is to your family."

"But what about teaching in a Christian school?" I ask. "I know God has called me to teach."

The pastor lays his hand over mine. "You will still teach. And you can influence even more people at a public school. It seems to me that this offer is from God and will allow you to provide for your family while Ron recovers."

I nod and shove the list of pros and cons into my purse.

"And what about you in all this?" he asks.

I shrug. "I'm okay."

He smiles. "That's what you always say. But you are taking on an enormous burden, Linda."

"Do I have a choice?" I respond.

He is quiet for a moment. "Yes," he says. "You have choices. None that I see you taking right now, but I want you to know that if this becomes too much for you someday in the future, if you tell me you just cannot manage this any longer, I will understand. I will not rebuke you."

Tears leak from my eyes. "But I would rebuke myself," I whisper.

He nods. "Then I will continue to pray for the strength and courage you will need."

Take a Moment

Take a moment to review God's promise against fear in Psalm 91:5–6, then write your responses to the questions that follow.

> *You will not fear the terror of the night, nor the arrow that flies by day, nor the pestilence that stalks in the darkness, nor the plague that destroys at midday. (Psalm 91:5–6)*

1. Can you think of a time when you made a caregiving decision out of fear or worry rather than faith?

____

____

____

____

____

2. What would it mean to you to fully step into God's shelter and trust him with the burdens you are carrying right now?

____

____

____

____

____

Prayer for Bravery

Lord, you are my light in the darkness. When the night feels long and my bed feels empty, remind me you are near, and help me be brave. Drive away fear with your perfect peace. Let your promises be my shield and let your love be my rest. I give you every worry I carry tonight. Wrap me in your protective wings and also watch over those I love. In Jesus' name, amen

CHAPTER 6

Staying Beside God

Verses for the Journey: A thousand may fall at your side, ten thousand at your right hand, but it will not come near you. You will only observe with your eyes and see the punishment of the wicked
(Psalm 91:7- 8)

From Linda's Journey

May 8, 2000
4:00 p.m.

We have settled back into the predictable routine of One North. Free from the pancreatic drain, Ron is beginning to look more like himself. Slowly, his healing pancreas is digesting lime gelatin and chicken broth. While the central feeding tube will remain in for a while longer, his vital signs are improving.

He is pale. Like legendary vampires, he has not seen the sun in a long time. We make his room cheerful. A

"Get Well Soon!" poster hangs on one wall, with the signatures of every student and teacher at Westtown Middle School. Each day, I tack up new cards from students, friends, and neighbors. Doctors and nurses come in to check the latest additions.

There are flowers, books, and treats that Ron cannot eat but shares with frequent visitors. Balloons bob on his bedrail. The infection is gone, his lungs are clear, and the chest drainage system has been moved to the aid of someone else.

Dr. Huffman, Joanne, comes in for her daily visit, admiring the cards on the wall and the fresh bouquet from our church. Kelvin from the manufacturing plant where Ron has worked for sixteen years, has been here and handed me an envelope with money collected from the guys on Ron's floor. Once again, I will be able to pay the mortgage. I make a mental note to send an email thanking them all. At least twenty people from the plant email me daily for updates.

Joanne checks Ron's vitals and his chart. She smiles. "I really think we can discuss discharging him. I want to monitor his lungs and do another X-ray tomorrow. We don't want another pneumonia relapse. Then, well, we'll see. Would a Friday release be good for you?"

I nod, already calculating logistics. "Will the visiting nurse come to our house on Saturday, or will we be on our own until Monday?"

"I'll let them know someone needs to come on the weekend. You'll also need to have someone stay with Ron while you're at work. And he can't use the stairs for the time being." She smiles at me. "But you're a teacher, so summer break is coming, right?"

I nod, my mind in overdrive. This is Wednesday. I have a conference with Allen's teacher tonight and a graduate class to attend tomorrow night. When will I find time to move the bed downstairs, prepare soft foods for Ron, call a church member to stay with him, and purchase a walker?

I sigh. Coming home will be a challenge for both of us. I will stay closely by my husband's side as we adapt, and God will stay by mine.

Rest in God's Protection

Psalm 34:7 says, "The angel of the Lord encamps around those who fear him, and he delivers them." Imagine that God has drawn a circle around you. Inside that circle, beside God, you are safe. No harm can touch you.

According to Psalm 91:7, "A thousand may fall at your side, ten thousand at your right hand, but it will not come near you." Even amid chaos, God's care is personal, intentional, and steady.

Close your eyes and breathe in and out. Envision a circle you can see around you, even if no one else can.

As you here draw a special circle of God's protection with you in the middle, pray for confidence in his care.

The months of caring for Ron's needs eventually slid into years. People would sometimes ask how I kept going. Honestly, I didn't always want to keep going. But I knew God had called me, as Ron's wife, to stay by his side even as God stayed by my side. I had peace in the middle of chaos. It was the peace that Jesus promised in John 16:33.

> *I have told you these things, so that in me you may have peace. In this world you will have trouble. But take heart! I have overcome the world.*

We cannot avoid life's sorrow or suffering, but we do not need to go through it alone. In difficult moments, we can encounter God's strength. His protection is not an escape, but we are never abandoned. God invites all, even those who sin against us, into his protective circle. The peace God gave me in hospital rooms was based not on knowing any outcome but on knowing God.

Relinquish your worries to God. Soak in his peace. Write here what you most fear and leave it in the circle of God's care.

____

____

____

____

____

Renew Through God's Word

It might not seem fair to you, but Scripture is clear: God wants us to extend his mercy to others, even those who have caused us pain. Choosing mercy over bitterness is part of staying in God's protective circle. First Timothy 2:1–4 tells us that showing mercy to others pleases God.

> *I urge then, first of all, that petitions, prayers, intercession and thanksgiving be made for all people—for kings and all those in authority, that we may live peaceful and quiet lives in all godliness and holiness. This is good, and pleases God our Savior, who wants all people to be saved and to come to a knowledge of the truth.*

When we hold on to unforgiveness, we often step outside the peace that God offers. My husband's injuries were caused by a careless truck driver who tried to run a red light. One moment of poor judgment changed everything for him and for my family. All my children struggled with anger. My oldest son, Dennis, carried the weight of anger the longest. God worked on his heart to help him see that accidents are rarely deliberate and that the man who hit Ron may have carried his own suffering. When Dennis told me he had forgiven the driver of the truck, I thought of Psalm 7:16.

The trouble they cause recoils on them; their violence comes down on their own heads.

We do not know the whole story of those who harm us, but we can trust that God sees every detail. Mercy makes room for peace and keeps us in God's protective circle. None of us is worthy of God's compassion and grace, but he freely gives it. We can extend it to others, too.

Do you need to forgive someone for your spouse's illness or accident? Forgiveness is often a journey. Print their name here and pray for them. If you're not yet ready to forgive, ask God to begin softening your heart.

Even in difficult circumstances, God can bring about good. During Ron's many hospital stays, visitors often left encouraged or renewed in their faith. In waiting rooms, my daughter and I had conversations with others about Jesus and hope.

Write one good thing that has come out of your loved one's current situation or that you hope might come from it.

____

____

____

____

____

Remember God's Faithfulness

When you choose to stay beside God, his protective circle surrounds your life much like water covers the body in baptism. The rite of baptism is one of the visible ways God marks us as his own. It is a promise that you belong to God and are safe in his care.

Whenever I witness a baptism, I remember God's promises to protect and guide me. I realize that baptism is not just applicable to one moment but becomes the ongoing reality of living in God's circle, a reality described in Isaiah 43:1b.

Do not fear, for I have redeemed you; I have summoned you by name; you are mine.

Even when we falter, God is still faithful to us, because we have been baptized into his care.

Reimagine your own baptism as placing you inside God's protective circle. Write down a caregiving challenge this imagining helps you trust to God now.

____

____

____

____

____

From Linda's Journey

May 8, 2000
9:00 p.m.

It is 9:00 p.m. when I thank Allen's caseworker, Cris, exuberantly for her time and leave the middle school. In the last months, Cris has often sent home a personal note, assuring me of her prayers for our family. I tell her I will pray for her and her new baby. She says she'll pray about Ron's discharge from the hospital tomorrow.

I cross the parking lot to my car, looking up at the night stars and marveling at the distant planets. God's work is displayed in brilliant detail before my weary eyes. I breathe deeply, thanking God that Ron's lungs are clear and that he will be home with his family soon.

"We made it," I say aloud.

But when I arrive home, there is a message in my daughter's careful handwriting on the pad by the phone. *Call Dr. Huffman at the hospital. Very important.* Joanne's beeper number follows.

Very important is underlined twice.

I let myself slide down to the floor as my heart sinks. Before I even call Joanne, I know Ron will not be coming home tomorrow.

After the call, I remind myself that even this disappointment is within God's circle of protection. God allowed Joanne to catch a returning infection before it became life-threatening. God's goodness is present, even in a circumstance that feels like defeat.

Take a Moment

Take a moment to sit quietly with the truth that when you stay beside God, he is always protecting you. Review Psalm 91:7–8, then write your responses to the questions that follow.

> *A thousand may fall at your side, ten thousand at your right hand, but it will not come near you. You will only observe with your eyes and see the punishment of the wicked (Psalm 91:7–8)*

1. What is one part of your caregiving life where you most need to feel God's protective care today?

2. What benefits do you feel you gain personally by living inside God's circle of care?

Prayer for God's Companionship

Dear God, thank you for your constant companionship, protection, and peace, even in the most challenging of circumstances. As I choose to rest in the circle of your care, to stay beside you and trust that you are greater than all the difficulties we face, help me remember you are with me, working in ways I cannot always see. Your steadfast presence will guide me each step of this journey. In Jesus' name, amen.

CHAPTER 7

Dwelling with the Most High

Verses for the Journey: If you say, "The Lord is my refuge," and you make the Most High your dwelling, no harm will overtake you, no disaster will come near your tent. (Psalm 91:9–10)

From Linda's Journey

May 12, 2000

3:00 p.m.

My friend's husband is going on a pilgrimage to Chartres Cathedral, where he intends to walk its famous stone labyrinth. Before leaving, Denis has been asking people to write on slips of paper the burdens they are carrying. He's putting them in his backpack, promising to stop at each turn of the labyrinth and pray for the burdens he carries with him.

A lot of the burdens he will carry are mine.

Ron is still in the hospital, back in intensive care again as he fights off the latest infection. Each day brings new tubes and additional problems. Seeing him is emotionally exhausting, and I wonder how any human being can recover from such damage. I am worn out and tired, dragging myself through each day at school, each visit to the hospital, each evening at home with the kids. It has occurred to me that these burdens may be mine to carry for a long time.

Bonnie is having a difficult semester at college, her mind always on her father. Allen is fearful at night, struggling to protect his mother and his sister from night terrors. The hammer remains under his bed, and he carefully checks the locks on each door and window at night.

I write all these burdens down and put them in Denis's backpack. I will remember and then relinquish them during his six days at Chartres. For six days, someone else can do the fretting and the worrying and the doubting.

Maybe I can find a small space for calm.

Asking myself why I worry, I remember God is in control. His refuge is not temporary but permanent. No matter how loudly the machines in the hospital beep or how heavy the burdens feel, I can dwell with God.

Jesus warned his disciples in Luke 21:34, "And take heed to yourselves, lest at any time your hearts be overcharged with surfeiting, and drunkenness, and cares of this life, and so that day come upon you unawares." (King James Version) As easily as I have slid the pieces of paper into Denis's backpack, I should be able to release them to Jesus.

When I continue to struggle and the burdens creep back into my heart, I will remind myself that I do not carry them alone. I do not dwell in the hospital or the waiting room. I dwell with God.

Rest in God's Protection

Here is where I would like to tell you I always trusted God 100 percent with what we were enduring after Ron's accident. But that is not the case. As one surgery led to another, Ron's stay in the hospital growing, I was often plagued with doubt, not only about my husband's recovery but about my ability to manage the journey.

I was tired. No, I was exhausted, all of my mental and physical resources depleted.

Are you depleted now, friend? Do you find yourself so tired that even the thought of a shower sounds like too much work?

Write "I just can't" and one task you need to do but lack the energy to complete. Then write "That's okay for now."

____

____

____

____

____

At this moment, you may be spending more time at the hospital than at home or may be caring for a loved one at home and unable to get out as often as you'd like. As a caregiver, you may be continually pushed out of your comfort zone. No physical location limits help from God, who invites us to live in his presence. Psalm 90:1 assures us that God can be our daily shelter.

Lord, you have been our dwelling place throughout all generations.

Even on occasions when I was away from the comfort of my little brick rowhouse, living out of a hospital tote bag, I was still at home with God. His presence traveled with me to many hospitals and rehabilitation centers and stayed by my side in waiting rooms. His invitation to dwell with him remained unchanged.

Write down a few ways the dwelling place of God can feel more like home than the temporary places where you have found yourself during caregiving.

Renew Through God's Word

Caregivers carry a huge burden. Even if we have family and friends around us, we often feel we are carrying the burden alone. If we are dwelling with God, we are never truly alone.

The Hebrew word used at Psalm 90:1 to mean "dwelling" is *ma'on*, which means "a habitation" or *"a place where you live."* Dwelling with God is about making your home in him. When we dwell with God, we stay with him, relying on him for strength, guidance, and peace, not just when things are hard, but every day.

As caregivers, it's easy to find ourselves dwelling in places of fear, worry, or exhaustion. But God invites us to live with him, a much better place to live. That doesn't mean physically escaping your caregiving role; it means placing your heart in God's care, even while you work and serve.

Psalm 84:1–2 speaks about closeness to God.

How lovely is your dwelling place, Lord Almighty! My soul yearns, even faints, for the courts of the Lord; my heart and my flesh cry out for the living God.

The writer of this psalm longed for God's presence the way we yearn for home after a tiring journey. Caregiving is a challenging journey. God invites you to find peace by living close to him, even when life is messy.

Psalm 31:20 identifies God's dwelling as a safe place.

> *In the shelter of your presence, you hide them from all human intrigues; you keep them safe in your dwelling from accusing tongues.*

Being close to God doesn't mean all our problems disappear, but it does mean that we are guarded and kept safe from destruction—even from the painful words or judgments of others who don't understand the weight we carry.

Even more than that, 2 Corinthians 5:1 makes clear that God's promise to dwell with us is not just for this life.

> *For we know that if the earthly tent we live in is destroyed, we have a building from God, an eternal house in heaven, not built by human hands.*

When we choose to dwell with God now, we're stepping into a relationship that stretches into eternity. His protection does not stop at the borders of this life but continues forever.

Write down whether you have been dwelling in fear or in God's presence today, then write where you want to dwell.

____

____

____

____

____

Remember God's Faithfulness

Notice that Psalm 91:9–10 is a conditional statement. The psalmist says, "If you say, 'The Lord is my refuge,' and you make the Most High your dwelling," then an action will follow. The command to make the Lord your refuge is repeated twice! Like a loving parent, God uses repetition in his promises to reinforce truth so it will settle deep in our hearts. He wants us to trust that his promises remain steady even when our circumstances change.

Just as you have repeated important statements to your children or as your parent has repeated instructions to you, God repeats his promises to us. His promises are always the same. They do not change day to day. Repeating them is one way God reminds us that he is trustworthy.

God also repeats his promises to make them clear. Perhaps you've had to say the same thing to a child again, but in a unique way. I was a teacher for thirty years, and my students often needed me to repeat something so that they could learn it. God, our Father, uses the same technique when repeating his promises to make them clear to us.

Write down why God's repeated promises of protection matter to you today.

____

____

____

____

____

Another reason God repeats his promises is due to the abundance of them. In Judaism, repetition often means plurality. There are many promises instead of just one. While the promises God makes to us in Psalm 91 are conditional on our acceptance of them, they are plentiful.

Write here at least one promise you find repeated in Psalm 91.

From Linda's Journey

May 25, 2000

1:00 p.m.

I can hear the voices of my students on the playground, shouting in the clear spring sunshine. Winter has finally loosened its grip, and now warmer days abound. I lean my head against the cool metal frame of a stall in the ladies' room, seeking comfort for my aching right eye.

My ophthalmologist reprimanded me for ignoring the ache when I finally visited his office yesterday. I've developed an infection in the transplanted cornea. I didn't tell him I've been practically living in a hospital for three months, with little time to take care of myself.

The recess bell rings, and I leave the relative calm of the restroom, heading down the hall to greet my students as they trickle in from the playground. I spy Phyllis, the principal, heading toward me with a dreaded pink slip in her hand, designating a message. As she moves closer, I see tears in her eyes.

An icy fear grips my heart, and I collapse against the wall. What now? I can't do this again.

Phyllis reaches out a hand and lays it on my arm. "I'll cover your class," she says as she shoves the pink slip into my hand. "You need to go."

What organ has broken? What infection has developed? What complication has arisen? I think of the chicken thighs I have put out on the kitchen counter to defrost; they will not be cooked tonight.

After I brace myself for the worst, I notice that, despite her tears, Phyllis is smiling. I glance at the slip in my hand and see Joanne's name at the bottom. Phyllis puts her arm around me.

"They're sending him home," she says. "He's finally coming home."

I drive to the hospital, rejoicing that my husband will soon be with his family. I know that the caregiving journey is not over. Many months of recovery remain. But I thank God for having brought us this far.

Take a Moment

Dwelling with God means living in his presence and resting in his care—even when the path is difficult. Reread Psalm 91:9–10 and write your responses to the questions that follow.

If you say, *"The Lord is my refuge," and you make the Most High your dwelling, no harm will overtake you, no disaster will come near your tent.* (Psalm 91:9–10).

1. Where have you been dwelling most often recently—in God's presence or in worry, fatigue, or fear?

____

____

____

____

____

2. What practical step can you take to invite God's presence more fully into your caregiving journey?

____

____

____

____

____

Prayer for Everlasting Hope

Lord, sometimes I find myself dwelling in worry, exhaustion, or fear—places that drain my spirit and steal my peace. But you invite me to dwell with you, in a refuge that never fades, in a home that holds me securely through every season. Help me to turn away from temporary dwellings that wear me down and to rest fully in your presence. May your peace settle deeply in my heart, and may your strength renew me each day. Thank you for being my unchanging refuge and my everlasting home. In Jesus' name, amen.

CHAPTER 8

Inviting Angel Guardians

Verses for the Journey: For he will command his angels concerning you to guard you in all your ways; they will lift you up in their hands, so that you will not strike your foot against a stone.
(Psalm 91:11–12)

From Linda's Journey

May 31, 2000
9:00 a.m.

Carefully dressed in gray sweatpants and a blue Phillies jacket, Ron shuffles into the elevator at church. We've timed our arrival during Sunday School so there are fewer people in the hallways to jostle his three-footed cane and pic lines.

Ron's progression up the center aisle of the church is painfully slow, but we are in no hurry. Bonnie, Allen, and I stand ready to assist Ron if needed, but he maneuvers himself into a seat without our help. He is too thin, I notice. And his skin has a waxy pallor to it.

"Here we are," he says as he looks around. "I've missed this place." He comments on the flowers on the altar, and I leave to get a bulletin for him. When I return, two deacons are heartily pumping his hands and patting him—gently—on his back.

"It is a miracle!" they both say. "To see you here, in one piece! God is good!"

I nod my head in agreement. God is good.

My water heater has sprung a leak, I can't sleep at night because Ron always needs something, and I have a final at graduate school on Tuesday for which I've not yet found time to study. But God is good.

Other people enter the sanctuary and want to speak to Ron, but the organist plays, so my children and I open our hymnals and stand for the first song. Ron stays seated, still too wobbly on his feet.

Pastor Lou has spotted us and smiles in our direction. "Before we begin today," he says, "I would like to offer a special prayer of thanks for God's graciousness in bringing our brother Ron back to us." Lou beams. "When I saw you there, Ron, I knew you were our own miracle. To see you here, in God's house, surrounded by your family, is proof of God's faithfulness."

I hardly hear the rest of the service; my mind is too tired to listen. After the final hymn, other well-wishers approach Ron, and two deacons offer to see him down on the elevator while I get the car. I am hurrying down the hallway when a hand lightly taps me on the arm.

"Linda," says Pastor Lou, "as wonderful as it is that Ron is home, I worry about you. Is this all too much for you?"

I panic for a moment; has Lou read my thoughts and seen into my soul? Then I realize he has probably only noticed the dark circles under my eyes and my fatigue.

"I'm a little tired," I admit. "But I'll be fine. School will be out soon, and I'll have time to recover." I give the pastor a bright smile. "The important thing is that Ron is home."

I can do this, I think as I pull the car up to the elevator exit. *I can do what's needed and express gratitude until I really am grateful Ron is home. I just need an angel to help me.*

Rest in God's Protection

There are angels around us all the time, not just in Christmas choirs. For spousal caregivers, that's good news. God knows how exhausting and overwhelming the caregiving role can be. He never intended for us to carry its burdens alone, so he assigned heavenly help for the long journey.

While the Bible does not tell us exactly when angels were created, Job 38:4–7 gives us a glimpse.

> *Where were you when I laid the earth's foundation? Tell me if you understand. Who marked off its dimensions? Surely you know! Who stretched a measuring line across it? On what were its footings set, or who laid its cornerstone—while the morning stars sang together and all the angels shouted for joy?*

Angels were already worshipping the Lord before there was an earth.

The word *angel* has origins in the Hebrew word *malach* and the Greek word *angelos*. Both those words mean "messengers," so one of the primary purposes of angels is to serve as messengers. Throughout Scripture, we find evidence of angels sent to deliver God's messages (see Genesis 19:1–15; 1 Kings 19:5–7; Daniel 10:10–15).

Angels are also "charged" with taking care of believers. The King James Bible uses the word charge in Psalm 91:11–12.

> *For he shall give his angels charge over thee, to keep thee in all thy ways. They shall bear thee up in their hands, lest thou dash thy foot against a stone.*

I didn't see angelic beings in my living room when Ron came home from the hospital, but I felt help when I needed it most. I was exhausted from juggling caregiving, graduate study, teaching at the middle school, and taking care of my family. In the chaos, God provided timely help and needed strength, sometimes in the form of friends who showed up with a meal, to do my laundry, or to drive Ron to an appointment in harsh weather.

God's provision does not mean that we should act foolishly and expect protection. We still need to follow the rules of safety. But when we walk with God, we can trust that he has provided us with the help we need. Sometimes that help may come through strangers, reminding us of Hebrews 13:2.

> *Do not forget to show hospitality to strangers, for by doing so some people have shown hospitality to angels without knowing it.*

Even when you don't feel protected, God's promises remain true. You are not alone in your caregiving journey. You are guarded by angels and loved by God.

Can you recall a moment when you experienced God's protection or unexpected help during your caregiving journey? Maybe it was a word of encouragement, a stranger's kindness, or a sense of strength you didn't think you had. Write down such a moment or what it means for you to know that God has assigned his angels to guard you today.

Renew Through God's Word

One way we can grow in confidence about God's angelic protection is by considering how he provided it to his people throughout Scripture. The Bible's true accounts remind us that God's care is personal, purposeful, and always right on time.

Daniel Gains Insight

At a low point in his life, Daniel experienced the comfort of an angel. When he feared the desolation of Israel because of the people's sins, he was granted understanding.

> *While I was speaking and praying, confessing my sin and the sin of my people Israel and making my request to the Lord my God for his holy hill—while I was still in prayer, Gabriel, the man I had seen in the earlier vision, came to me in swift flight about the time of the evening sacrifice. He instructed me and said to me, "Daniel, I have*

now come to give you insight and understanding." (Daniel 9:20–22)

Write down a caregiving topic for which you are seeking insight and understanding.

____

____

____

____

____

Elijah Receives Bread and Water

Elijah, one of God's great prophets, found himself utterly worn out physically, emotionally, and spiritually. Fleeing from the threat of death by Queen Jezebel, Elijah reached a breaking point. He lay down under a bush, ready to give up. But God sent an angel to provide exactly what Elijah needed in that moment.

> *Then he lay down under the bush and fell asleep. All at once an angel touched him and said, "Get up and eat." He looked around, and there by his head was some bread baked over hot coals, and a jar of water. He ate and drank and then lay down again. (1 Kings 19:5)*

Write down a provision you presently need.

____

____

____

____

____

Peter Follows

The New Testament gives another striking example of angelic rescue. After King Herod arrested Peter, it looked like the apostle's end, but God had other plans. Church members prayed for Peter while he was in prison, and an angel of the Lord appeared to him.

> *Suddenly an angel of the Lord appeared and a light shone in the cell. He struck Peter on the side and woke him. "Quick, get up!" he said, and the chains fell off Peter's wrists. Then the angel said to him, "Put on your clothes and sandals." And Peter did so. "Wrap your cloak around you and follow me," the angel told him. (Acts 12:7–8)*

Notice that the actions the angel required of Peter were simple yet exhibited faith. Praying for angelic help for caregiving can also be a simple act of faith.

Write down your feelings about praying for angelic help for caregiving.

Jesus Is Attended

Even Jesus experienced the comfort of angels. After his exhausting forty days of fasting and facing Satan's temptations, God sent help.

> *Then the devil left him, and angels came and attended him. (Matthew 4:11)*

Write down a temptation you are facing in your caregiving life.

Claiming Your Angel Story

In each Bible story just referenced, God provided angelic help exactly when it was needed. As caregivers, you can hold fast to that same promise: you are guarded by angels. You might not always recognize them, but their presence is real. They are guarding, guiding, protecting, and encouraging you in each step of your caregiving journey.

As you write down an area in your caregiving journey where you most need God's help now, trust that he—the same God who sent angels to Elijah, Daniel, Peter, and even Jesus—is watching over you today.

____

____

____

____

____

Remember God's Faithfulness

The Old and New Testaments mention angels almost three hundred times. God wants to take care of us, and the ministrations of angels are among the many ways he does so. We read of the might and obedience of angels at Psalm 103:20.

Praise the Lord, you his angels, you mighty ones who do his bidding, who obey his word.

Your situation as a caregiver might look very bleak to you right now, but God has given angels authority to act on your behalf, to free you from ineffective worry and self-effort. God created angels specifically to help you.

Angels are examples to us. They obey and worship God without ceasing, offering us a glimpse of unbroken devotion. Scripture gives us a striking image of their awe-filled reverence in Isaiah 6:2–3.

> *Above him were seraphim, each with six wings: With two wings they covered their faces, with two they covered their feet, and with two they were flying. And they were calling to one another: "Holy, holy, holy is the Lord Almighty; the whole earth is full of his glory."*

As caregivers, we may not always have the strength to sing or soar, but we can follow the example of the angels by turning our hearts toward obedience and worship, especially in those private, troubled moments of the caregiving journey.

The Bible not only tells us about the past actions of angels but also gives us hope for what is to come. We are told that when Jesus returns, he will be accompanied by powerful angels, bringing justice to those who have suffered.

God is just. He will pay back trouble to those who trouble you and give relief to you who are troubled, and to us as well. This will happen when the Lord Jesus is revealed from heaven in blazing fire with his powerful angels. (2 Thessalonians 1:6–7) If you're weary from carrying more than your share of burdens, take heart. God has not forgotten you. A day is coming when all things will be made right. His comfort will reach into the deepest places of your exhaustion.

Write down one circumstance in which you need intervention and comfort now, then pray that God will give you what you need.

____

____

____

____

____

From Linda's Journey

August 27, 2000
10:00 a.m.

Before leaving his disciples and returning to heaven, Jesus said he would bring them peace, but "not as the world brings peace." I wonder now what they thought about Jesus' conditional promise. There were those among them who thought their rabbi had come to free them from Roman rule and establish an earthly peace, bringing rest to their weary bodies and spirits. But in those last words, Jesus clarified that his brand of peace was not something the world could give or even understand.

I cling to that peace now, desperately grabbing it with ragged fingernails. Once again, I am sitting in the fourth-floor waiting room of the hospital, anxious for the surgeon to come out and tell me that Ron's latest operation is over. What should have been a relatively minor procedure to repair a hernia has been complicated by infections and previous scarring.

Today, I am alone. Dennis has moved back to his college apartment. Bonnie is at her job at the day care; I did not call her. Allen is at home, and while he offered to come with me, I know hospitals frighten him.

After I flip through the book I have brought to read, I rummage in my knitting bag for a project. What I really need, though, is not distraction but calm. I close my eyes and pray for strength. For peace. For comfort.

"Excuse me," says a small voice at my side. "I hate to interrupt you."

My eyes snap open. "Is the surgery finished?" I look up at a diminutive gray-haired woman in a pink hospital smock, one of the volunteers.

The woman shakes her head. "I don't know. But I noticed you've been here a while, and I thought maybe you could use a little something."

In her hand is a foam cup, a tea bag hanging from its side. I take the warm drink gratefully.

"I don't even know how you like it," she says, pulling creamer cups and sugar packets from her smock pocket. "Maybe you don't even drink tea."

I smile at this little angel God has sent. "But I do," I assure her. "And it's just what I need. Thank you."

"Bless you," she says.

I put the cup on a nearby table and add one cream and one sugar. I look up to thank her again, but she's gone.

Ron's surgery lasts another two hours, and I never see the gray-haired woman in the pink smock again. I don't know for sure, but I like to think that woman was an angel, sent to comfort me in a moment of need.

Write down a brief description of a moment when someone, human or heavenly, showed up right when you needed guarding or comfort.

____

____

____

____

____

Take a Moment

Psalm 91:11–12 assures us of angelic help. Take a few moments to reread and reflect on the verses, then write your responses to the questions that follow.

> *For he will command his angels concerning you to guard you in all your ways; they will lift you up in their hands, so that you will not strike your foot against a stone. (Psalm 91:11–12)*

1. Think back on your caregiving journey. Have there been moments when you sensed God's protection or unexpected help?

2. Angels ministered to Elijah's physical needs. How might an angel minister to a physical need you have today?

Prayer for Angelic Help

Father, thank you for assigning angels to guard me. When I feel tired and unseen, remind me that I am never truly alone. Help me trust that you have already sent help in response to my prayers. The help is sometimes visible, sometimes not. I know that angels are real and surround me even now. They will help me in my caregiving journey. In Jesus' name, amen.

CHAPTER 9

Treading on Trouble

Verse for the Journey: You will tread on the lion and the cobra; you will trample the great lion and the serpent. (Psalm 91:13)

From Linda's Journey

September 14, 2000

7:00 p.m.

I am in a graduate class doing a presentation on Native American literature when my new cell phone rings. The sound, still foreign to me, is startling. The professor frowns.

"It has to be an emergency," I say. "Only my kids have the number, and they know I'm in class."

Dr. Beeghly nods. I was in her class last semester, when Ron was injured. "Take it in the hallway," she says quietly.

I step into the hall, my heart pounding, my palms beginning to sweat. "Hello?"

"It's Dad," my daughter says without preamble. We are, sadly, used to calls like this. "His incision split open. He's bleeding pretty badly. We're on our way to the emergency room."

I gulp, wondering how my slender daughter will get her six-foot-two-inch father into her car. It seems we are all learning to do things we once might've thought impossible.

"He's pretty dizzy," she reports. "I already called Dr. Huffman. She'll meet us at the hospital."

Smart girl. I can be grateful for the lessons my children are learning, if not for the reasons. "I'll meet you there."

"No hurry," she assures me. "I've got it under control. Allen is gathering Dad's medications and some snacks."

Once again, I marvel at the resourcefulness of my children, who have learned the procedure for trips to the emergency room: take the meds, snacks, and change for the pay phone. When did my daughter become so calm in a crisis?

I push End on my cell phone and return to the classroom. "I have to go," I tell Dr. Beeghly. "My daughter is taking my husband to the emergency room." I pick up my presentation materials. "I'll finish this, though."

"No," she says kindly. "Just go."

I nod. "I can finish it next week."

"You're done," she says. "You've got your A. Go take care of your husband." She smiles. "And God bless you."

I cannot help but question God as I drive down Route 202 and head to the all-too-familiar hospital. Why has he allowed Ron to suffer like this? Hasn't the poor man been through enough? Haven't we all been through enough? I drive in silence, waiting for God to answer me.

The hospital lights blur against the car windshield as I pull into the parking lot. Dr. Huffman has already seen Ron by the time I hurry into the examining room. The lines in her face deepen with concern. "I was afraid of this," she says. "The walls of his abdomen are just too weak right now. We've stopped the bleeding, and he's getting a transfusion. Tomorrow or the next day, we'll put in a mesh wall." She touches my shoulder. "This will not be easy, Linda."

I nod. *What else is new?*

Another unknown. Another battle. Another path I didn't choose but will have to walk anyway.

It is once again the early hours of the morning when Bonnie, Allen, and I leave the hospital. We've become night owls, trained by circumstance, familiar with emergency room routines, but not immune to weariness. Tomorrow I'll need to come back with clothes and comforts for Ron. I'll need to get a substitute for my class.

Another surgery. Another recovery. Another stretch of unknown ground under my feet.

God hasn't answered the questions I shouted into the car's silence. But as I sit behind the wheel in the dark parking lot and turn the key in the ignition, a small whisper rises somewhere beneath the weight of my fear. I say it aloud to convince myself of its truth.

"God can tread over our enemies. He can do this."

Rest in God's Protection

For a caregiver, rest doesn't mean retreat. There is always another battle. Have you reached the point where you're wondering if God has forgotten about you? When troubles just keep coming, it's easy to believe you've been left alone. But even in the hardest moments, God is still in control. Even Jesus walked through sorrow, betrayal, and pain, treading on spiritual trouble to secure our peace.

We are reminded of God's promise of peace in Isaiah 26:3.

> *You will keep in perfect peace those whose minds are steadfast, because they trust in you.*

Sometimes, any peace can feel just out of reach. Illness, surgeries, and constant unwelcome news can pull a caregiver's thoughts in a hundred directions. But those things are happening around you, not inside you. In your spirit, God is still at work.

Psalm 91:13 reminds us of his protection.

You will tread on the lion and the cobra; you will trample the great lion and the serpent. Think about lions—bold, strong, roaring creatures with massive jaws. Just like a serious illness or another surgery, they can seem overwhelming. And cobras—stealthy creatures that strike without warning—are like those unexpected emergencies that shake caregivers to the core. But we are not helpless.

You are not alone. Psalm 91:13 is not daring us to fight wild beasts; it's showing us what God can do. He gives us the strength to *walk over* what threatens us. God's protection lets us tread where we once thought we would fall.

Scripture makes this promise clear.

No, in all these things we are more than conquerors through him who loved us. (Romans 8:37)

The God of peace will soon crush Satan under your feet. The grace of our Lord Jesus be with you. (Romans 16:20)

With God's help, we don't just survive. We overcome.

To tread is to march over. To trample is to crush beneath your feet. Picture yourself treading over every fear and worry. Imagine crushing Satan's attempts to steal your peace. His defeat is already written in Revelation 12:9.

The great dragon was hurled down—that ancient serpent called the devil, or Satan, who leads the whole world astray. He was hurled to the earth, and his angels with him.

Do not let Satan lead you astray into fear, doubt, and unrest. Keep your heart and mind focused on God.

Copy Isaiah 26:3 here, accepting each word as the promise that you can rest in God's protection.

____

____

____

____

____

Renew Through God's Word

During my husband's long illnesses, I often wrestled with doubts about God's protection and power. I remember sitting in yet another waiting room after Ron's bleeding emergency, anxious and filled with fear as he was prepared for surgery. Yet, even in that moment of uncertainty, I saw glimpses of God's care.

My children, Bonnie and Allen, knew exactly what to do to get Ron help. They'd made the right calls. Dr. Huffman was on call that night, able to care for Ron. Despite the setback, Ron remained in good spirits before surgery. Those glimpses of God's protection stayed with me through the procedure and beyond.

Write down an evidence of God's protection and power you have seen in your caregiving situation.

____

____

____

____

____

When Jesus sent out seventy-two disciples to spread his message, they returned amazed to have seen even demons submitting to the name of Christ. Jesus told them,

> *I have given you authority to trample on snakes and scorpions and to overcome all the power of the enemy; nothing will harm you. However, do not rejoice that the spirits submit to you, but rejoice that your names are written in heaven. (Luke 10:19–20)*

These words of Jesus remind us that we are not powerless. As caregivers, we walk on difficult terrain, but our names are known in heaven.

Print your name here and rejoice, knowing it is written in heaven.

____

We also have the gift of the Holy Spirit, promised to us by Jesus before his ascension.

> *Very truly I tell you, whoever believes in me will do the works I have been doing, and they will do even greater things than these, because I am going to the Father. (John 14:12)*

You are not walking through this caregiving journey on your own. The Holy Spirit breathes life into you. He makes you resilient, gives you hope, and transforms your heart day by day.

You might be thinking, "Believing in these promises requires more faith than I have. I'm overwhelmed, and I just can't believe God is in control." I understand, because I've been there—discouraged, heart heavy, and struggling to hold on to faith.

But we don't need an enormous amount of faith to see God at work. Even a small measure that Jesus compared to the size of a small mustard seed is enough.

He replied, "Because you have so little faith. Truly I tell you, if you have faith as small as a mustard seed, you can say to this mountain, 'Move from here to there' and it will move. Nothing will be impossible for you." (Matthew 17:20)

If you've ever eaten pickles, you've probably seen mustard seeds floating in the jar. Those tiny seeds grow into large bushes that can reach over three feet tall. Your faith may feel small, but it matters to God.

Here, draw a tiny mustard seed or write a few words about the size of one as a reminder of the faith you carry—even if it feels small right now.

____

____

____

____

____

Remember God's Faithfulness

Treading on trouble doesn't always look like victory. Sometimes, it looks like holding onto faith in the dark. I've never stepped on a lion or serpent, but I've had to step over fear, doubt, exhaustion, and questions with no easy answers. That, too, is spiritual treading.

Like many caregivers, I've wrestled with doubts and sorrows as my husband's illnesses dragged on and our prayers for healing seemed unanswered. God sometimes chooses not to heal in the way we hope. He chose not to heal Ron fully. But he gave us another promise in Romans 8:18.

> *I consider that our present sufferings are not worth comparing with the glory that will be revealed in us.*

My faith grew strongest during the hardest seasons, expanding from a small mustard seed-sized into something much larger and stronger. The years of caregiving helped to shape me; my trials were not wasted but made me stronger. Romans 5:3–4 presents the products of suffering.

Not only so, but we also glory in our sufferings, because we know that suffering produces perseverance; perseverance, character; and character, hope.

Choosing among faith, perseverance, character, and hope, write down at least one product of suffering growing in you during your difficult season of caregiving.

____

____

____

____

____

If God chooses not to heal your loved one in this life, you can rest in the greater hope he promises. Speaking of Christ, Paul reminds us in Philippians 3:21 that transformation awaits beyond this world.

> *Who, by the power that enables him to bring everything under his control, will transform our lowly bodies so that they will be like his glorious body.*

God is faithful and unchanging. You may not understand his timing, but you can trust his heart to remain steady even when everything else in your life is unstable. Hebrews 13:8 assures us of the unchanging character of Jesus.

Jesus Christ is the same yesterday and today, and forever.

We experience the constancy of Jesus in our lives every day, even on days we only notice it in the sunrise.

Write down one way you experienced the steady constancy of Jesus in your life.

____

____

____

____

____

____

From Linda's Journey

October 1, 2000

9:30 p.m.

My grandmother taught me to knit when I was nine. My first attempt was a disaster: a brown scarf for my father full of dropped stitches and uneven rows. But my father wore that scarf proudly, never once pointing out its flaws. He knew it was just the beginning and that I would improve with practice.

The image of loose ends slowly being woven back together returns to me during one of my hardest caregiving tasks.

Ron has been home from the hospital for two weeks now. The open wound from his last surgery is slowly healing, as the edges of skin knit themselves together. The first time I saw the wound—and realized I would need to clean and dress it—I had to steady myself by grabbing the dresser next to his bed. It was a raw, red, gaping hole. The sight of it terrified me. I took a deep breath.

"Give me a minute," I told Ron. "I'll do it, but I need to get myself ready." The responsibility of tending to it three times a day felt impossible. How could I do this?

But over time, I learned. Now I can change the dressing in two minutes. I lay out everything ahead of time: saline, gauze, surgical tape, gloves. Redressing the wound has become a practiced routine—one hand removing the old bandage, the other cleaning and covering.

The horror of the wound has slowly been replaced by wonder at how God designed our bodies to heal. Surely only a kind Father could have created such detail and care.

I'm not sure I can call myself grateful yet, but I am learning to see his power in the small, daily things.

Take a Moment

You will probably never be asked to tread over lions and cobras as mentioned in Psalm 91:13, but there are many troubles a caregiver may encounter. Reread the verse then write your responses to the questions that follow.

> *You will tread on the lion and the cobra; you will trample the great lion and the serpent. (Psalm 91:13)*

1. What trouble in your caregiving life has felt too big for you to manage alone? How has God met you in that trouble, or how are you hoping he will?

____

____

____

____

____

2. What aspects of this difficult season of caregiving have shaped your faith, strength, or perseverance?

____

____

____

____

____

3. What promise of God can you hold on to as you continue to face each day?

____

____

____

____

____

Prayer for Overcoming

Father God, you know the troubles of my caregiving life and how small I feel beneath their weight. Thank you, by your strength, I can tread on and overcome what once terrified me. When doubt creeps into my mind or heart, remind me of your promises. Help me trust you even when I can't see my way forward. Give me courage to trample every trouble beneath my feet, knowing you walk with me. In Jesus' name, amen.

CHAPTER 10

Finding Courage in God's Rescue

Verse for the Journey: "Because he loves me," says the Lord, "I will rescue him; I will protect him, for he acknowledges my name." (Psalm 91:14)

From Linda's Journey

October 7, 2000

11:00 a.m.

"What I've learned from my parents is the meaning of the word courage."

Allen's voice trembles just a little as he stands in front of the packed church, microphone in hand. Today, Ron and I are celebrating our twenty-fifth wedding anniversary, an occasion that recently felt out of reach. Only weeks ago, Ron was in the hospital again, and the weight of caregiving was heavy. But somehow, with God's help, we have made it to this day.

"What really matters isn't money, or where you live, or how much you have. It's love." Allen turns toward us and wipes a tear from his eye. "Thanks, Mom and Dad, for showing me that. For letting me be me. For letting me grow. For teaching me that you don't have to understand everything—you just have to trust God's love and have courage."

I blink back tears as I listen to my son's words. He doesn't know the full weight of what these last eight months have held, how many times I've cried in parking lots or sat quietly by Ron's hospital bed, praying without words. There were moments I did not think we would make it through our challenges. God's rescue did not involve a miracle but delivered help, peace, and timely provision.

Bonnie and Dennis echo thoughts similar to Allen's when they take turns at the microphone. They haven't been handed life on a silver platter. They won't receive luxury trips or fancy graduation presents. They might get a watch if we can swing it. But I pray we've given them something much better: the courage to trust God even when life doesn't make sense, because God is in the rescue business.

The trials of these twenty-five years of marriage—miscarriages, job loss, illness, financial strain, deaths—have required more courage and faith than my little mustard seeds of either. I wouldn't have chosen any of those trials. But God's steady hands have carried us through every valley. What we have gained is greater than anything we have lost.

I consider just a few of God's gifts for my children:

- Strength that doesn't collapse under pressure
- Faith that looks up when the road ahead is uncertain
- Perseverance born in the fire of difficulty

These are treasures no thief can steal and no decay can touch.

Given the choice between worldly wealth or what Allen spoke of today, I'd choose courage rooted in God's rescue every time.

Rest in God's Protection

Verse 14 of Psalm 91 marks a shift in voice. Instead of the psalmist speaking about God, now God is speaking to us.

> *"Because he loves me," says the Lord, "I will rescue him; I will protect him, for he acknowledges my name."*

More than a comfort, God's pronouncement is a personal promise rooted in our relationship with him.

God's rescue is not always dramatic, but it is always rooted in love. He sees you. He comes near you. When caregiving challenges mount, it's natural to ask, "Why isn't God doing more to stop these troubles?" But often, God's rescue shows up not as a way out, but as a way through. Because of his provision, we receive one more hour of strength, an unexpected word of encouragement, and a check that arrives just in time.

He answers our call, and we continue on, not because we become fearless, but because we are no longer alone. Through Psalm 91:14, God gives caregivers four particular rescue promises that give us strength for the caregiving journey.

He Rescues Through His Presence

God doesn't promise to remove all trouble, but he does promise to be with us always. He shows up in the ICU, for midnight prayers, and on lonely drives home. Deuteronomy 31:8 assures us of God's continual presence.

> *The Lord himself goes before you and will be with you; he will never leave you nor forsake you. Do not be afraid; do not be discouraged.*

During Ron's illness, he was in twelve different hospitals. God was in every single one.

He Rescues by Giving Strength

We often reach the end of our own strength before a trial ends. God can provide us with the strength we need at any moment. When my weariness from caregiving seemed to be too much, I found truth in the promise of Isaiah 40:29.

> *He gives strength to the weary and increases the power of the weak.*

Some days, just walking from the parking garage at the hospital to Ron's room required more strength than I thought I had. God continued to provide me with strength in small portions, just enough to take the next step.

He Rescues by Guarding Our Souls

God promises to guard our souls and bring us safely through earthly life. At 2 Timothy 4:18, we find promises of both rescue and safety.

> *The Lord will rescue me from every evil attack and will bring me safely to his heavenly kingdom. To him be glory forever and ever.*

He Rescues Through the Cross

God's greatest provision was salvation through Jesus Christ. We are promised eternal security in God's love. My husband's favorite verse is John 3:16, and it and the two verses following make those eternal promises clear.

> *For God so loved the world that he gave his one and only Son, that whoever believes in him shall not perish but have eternal life. For God did not send his Son into the world to condemn the world, but to save the world through him. Whoever believes in him is not condemned, but whoever does not believe stands condemned already because they have not believed in the name of God's one and only Son. (John 3:16–18)*

Every caregiver needs to know that eternal promises are not abstract. They ensure tangible expressions of God's love here and now. They could mean a moment of peace, a second wind, a doctor who listens, or a verse that breathes needed strength.

Choosing among God's presence, strength, soul-protecting care, and eternal provision, write down a promise from God that you most need to claim right now.

____

____

____

____

____

Renew Through God's Word

God's rescue does not mean he changes our circumstances. Often, he changes us from the inside out. When your life as a caregiver feels out of control, courage begins with surrender, not effort. You probably won't be able to choose what happens to your loved one, but you can choose how you respond.

There are three choices you can make that will build your courage in the midst of trouble and chaos. These three choices—trust, attitude, and action—can help you build courage wherever you are.

Trust His Rescue (Even When You Don't Understand)

Trust is built slowly, often through hard experiences. Caregiving stretches our faith because so much that we are facing is uncertain. Even when we cannot see the outcome of the latest surgery or the latest medical test, we can trust the heart of God who rescues. Proverbs 3:5–6 tells us that we should trust not in our own thoughts but in God's ways.

> *Trust in the Lord with all your heart and lean not on your own understanding; in all your ways submit to him, and he will make your paths straight.*

Write down a caregiving area you have tried to manage by leaning on your own understanding and are now ready to entrust to God.

Fix Your Eyes on God

Your attitude is shaped by where you fix your gaze. As caregivers, we can seldom see beyond what needs to be done in the moment. God sees the whole picture. News from the operating room may cause us to despair, but keeping our eyes on Jesus will help our courage grow. First John 4:4 assures us that Jesus is more powerful than any unwelcome news.

> *You, dear children, are from God and have overcome them, because the one who is in you is greater than the one who is in the world.*

Fear may still whisper, but courage will grow when you focus on God's strength instead of your struggle. I can't say my husband and I were never afraid, but our son Allen saw courage in us because we chose to keep our eyes on God, whose strength was greater than all our troubles.

Write down one of your caregiving fears or struggles, then write and circle "God's strength" above it.

Take Quiet, Courageous Action

Often in caregiving, quiet and unseen action was powerful. When Ron was recovering from surgery, I couldn't fix what had broken. But I could choose to pray, to knit, to sit beside him with an open Bible in my hand. Expressions of trust in God's rescue, these quiet or unseen acts of love gave me courage. I chose to allow God control of my mind, as Romans 12:2 encourages us to do.

> *Do not conform to the pattern of this world, but be transformed by the renewing of your mind. Then you will be able to test and approve what God's good will is—his good, pleasing and perfect will.*

Write down a quiet action you might take to express your trust in God's rescue.

Remember God's Faithfulness

God's promises in Psalm 91:14 call us to a courageous love that endures, even when everything is falling apart. The prophet Habakkuk models such love of God.

> *Though the fig tree does not bud, and there are no grapes on the vines, though the olive crop fails and the fields produce no food, though there are no sheep in the pen and no cattle in the stalls, yet I will rejoice in the lord, I will be joyful in God my Savior. (Habakkuk 3:17–18)*

Because we love and acknowledge God, even in loss, he responds with protection and rescue. We don't rejoice in trials as if everything is fine. We rejoice because God is still God. His promises to us have not changed but are steady, even when life isn't. God's faithful promises for us are threefold.

His love remains.

His Word is trustworthy.

His rescue is real, even if it doesn't come right away.

God promises to be with us in every circumstance. Just as he was faithful to Abraham in good times and bad (Genesis 15:6), God is faithful to us now. First Peter 5:7 tells us what we can do with the anxiety we carry.

Cast all your anxiety on him because he cares for you.

As a caregiver, you may have moments when you feel exhausted—physically, emotionally, and spiritually. In those moments, God's strength sustains you. Unlike friends who need rest, God surrounds us with a presence that never fades. We may experience it as a feeling of peace or strength, a quiet whisper, or a flicker of light in the dark.

Write down at least one of God's faithful promises that you feel can strengthen your courage when life feels overwhelming.

From Linda's Journey

November 20, 2000
6:30 p.m.

The hospital has become all too familiar again. Ron's wound now harbors three types of bacteria, requiring multiple rounds of antibiotics on top of the thrice-daily dressing changes. There will be another surgery, including a skin graft and a long recovery.

It feels overwhelming, but can it really be worse than what we've already faced? And even if it is, God's rescue has carried me through before.

As I'm about to leave Ron's hospital room, Joanne pulls me into a hug. "Your anniversary service was lovely," she says softly. "I was honored you invited me." She pauses, then adds, "I know this is a lot. But I also know you can do this. I saw the faith you and your children have in God. No matter what happens, you're going to be okay."

Her words spark a flicker of courage in my weary heart. The journey isn't easy, but God's goodness remains constant. He will rescue us again and again, in his faithful way. As Jesus, who shepherds me, said, "*The one who sent me is with me; he has not left me alone, for I always do what pleases him*" (John 8:29).

In the face of uncertainty and exhaustion, courage comes from trusting that God's love holds me steady. His presence strengthens me when I feel weak, and his faithfulness gives me hope beyond what I can see. His rescue is already underway.

God is still with me.

God is still good.

God still rescues.

Take a Moment

This chapter explored the courage we can find in the rescue God promises at Psalm 91:14. Take a moment to reread the verse, then write your responses to the questions that follow.

> *"Because he loves me," says the Lord, "I will rescue him; I will protect him, for he acknowledges my name." (Psalm 91:14)*

1. During this season of caregiving, where have you experienced God's rescue or strengthening?

____

____

____

____

____

2. When you feel worn down or afraid, what helps you hold on to God's promises?

____

____

____

____

____

3. How might your daily actions reflect the courage that comes from knowing you are loved and rescued by God?

____

____

____

____

____

Prayer for Courage

Lord, thank you for loving me with a love that reaches down and lifts me up. When I feel weak, remind me that I have courage because of your love, and anchor me in the strength of your presence. Help me trust you even when I do not understand the way forward. Let your faithful rescue give me the courage to keep going today and the peace to rest in you tomorrow. In Jesus' name, amen.

CHAPTER 11

Calling on God for Answers

Verse for the Journey: He will call on me, and I will answer him; I will be with him in trouble, I will deliver him and honor him. (Psalm 91:15)

From Linda's Journey

December 22, 2000

11:00 p.m.

I sit at the kitchen table, looking over the letter I've just written and printed to include with this year's Christmas cards. How do you put almost an entire year of hospitals, surgeries, and disappointments into a cheerful Christmas greeting? I need to trust that somehow the words will show what I most want to tell our friends and family: we called on God many times this year, and he always answered us, though not always as we expected.

I hear Allen behind me in the living room, shifting the few presents beneath my grandmother's little ceramic tree. It is the only Christmas tree we will have. My son's voice is soft but steady. "Dad always made sure we had a lot of gifts," he mumbles. I feel the sharp contrast between this Christmas and the ones before. There will be no last-minute surprise gift from Ron, no over-the-top generosity that defied our budget but delighted the kids.

"At least your dad will be home for Christmas," I tell Allen, my voice a mixture of hope and doubt. I pray it's true. Ron's current hospital stay has already been five days longer than predicted.

When Allen retreats to his room and his video games, I return my attention to the letter.

Dear Friends,

I've been searching for the Wise Men this Christmas. On our first "married" Christmas, Ron gave me a white porcelain set of the Holy Family. Every year, he attempted to complete the set, but it was discontinued, so there are no shepherds or Magi at our Nativity scene.

I thought about the long journey of the Magi this past week. It could not have been easy. There were no four-star hotels along the way to ease the weariness of their travels. But they continued, night after night, mile after mile, with only a Star and a promise to guide them.

Our family has been on our own difficult journey this year. Beginning with Ron's accident on March 1, we have trodden unexpected paths through mountains and valleys. There were many moments when we wondered if we would ever walk into the light again. But we kept on walking, guided by the light of Jesus and His promise to us: "I will never leave you nor forsake you."

The journey of the Wise Men ended when they reached the Child and "fell down and worshipped Him" (Matthew 2:11). They departed back to their own countries, defying wicked Herod, and they are not mentioned again in the Gospels. I believe they were changed forever by the journey.

Our own journey has not yet ended. In the weeks, months, and years ahead, Ron will continue to heal. There may be other complications. My family will continue to trust in the strength God has given us in the last nine months.

The Wise Men did not turn back from their journey until they had reached their final desti-

nation. Perhaps next year, we, too, will stand in awe before the newborn King and rest from our travails. We pray many blessings upon you this Holy Season and rejoice in knowing that, in some small ways, our lives have touched yours.

Ron, Linda, Dennis, Bonnie, and Allen

Satisfied with the letter, I fold printed copies carefully, then tuck them and the Christmas cards into envelopes and begin to seal each one.

I want our friends to know what God has done, not because the story is finished, but because the journey is still going. God is still guiding us. As I seal the last envelope, I pray for the strength to keep going.

Rest in God's Protection

God's desire is to rescue His people. Danger and trials are still part of our human lives, even when we honor God. Jesus reminded His disciples of this truth with powerful words.

I have told you these things, so that in me you may have peace. In this world you will have trouble. But take heart! I have overcome the world. (John 16:33)

Though troubles come, Jesus is greater than anything in this world. He protects us in troubling times, for a reason expressed beautifully in Psalm 18:17–19.

He rescued me from my powerful enemy, from my foes, who were too strong for me.

They confronted me in the day of my disaster, but the Lord was my support.

He brought me out into a spacious place; he rescued me because he delighted in me.

The Hebrew word used for God's delight in Psalm 18 is *hepes*; its meaning is "to incline, to bend toward." Just as a grandparent might bend down to a beloved grandchild, God bends down to us.

Think of something that you delight in, then write down how you feel knowing that, given God's great capacities, your delight is just a fraction of how much God delights in you.

____

____

____

____

____

God's delight in you doesn't mean your life will be easy, but it does mean you will never be forgotten in the struggle. You may feel that your enemy is too powerful now. Fear, illness, discouragement, and burnout stalk you on a daily basis. The biblical Job also experienced a boatload of trouble. When it seemed things couldn't get worse for him, they did. God heard and responded to Job's complaints.

I often felt as troubled as Job during my husband's prolonged illness. Just as Ron recovered from one problem, such as an infection, another problem would arise—with his pancreas, his liver, or his lungs. To cope with the onslaught of trouble, I needed moments of rest in the knowledge that, no matter what happened, God delighted in Ron and me. Romans 8:28 helped me remember.

> *And we know that in all things God works for the good of those who love him, who have been called according to his purpose.*

Often, we need to change our perspective amid our trials. Our troubles may not seem like a gift to us, for example, but our experiences can help us comfort others in their trials. We can do so because we receive comfort from God, "who comforts us in all our troubles, so that we can comfort those in any trouble with the comfort we ourselves receive from God" (2 Corinthians 1:4).

Resting in God's protection means trusting him even when answers aren't clear. It means choosing prayer and God's peace over worry.

List a few spiritual practices or daily activities that might help you lean more fully on God's peace.

____

____

____

____

____

Renew Through God's Word

When we're worn down by caregiving and trials, it sometimes helps to slow down and closely study a Bible promise filled with powerful actions between God and those who call on him in times of trouble. Psalm 91:15 contains such a promise.

Take a moment to write your own paraphrase or response for each of the following phrases drawn from Psalm 91:15. There are no right or wrong responses. Let this be your personal conversation with God's Word.

He will call on me: ________________________

I will answer him: ________________________

I will be with him in trouble: ________________

I will deliver him: ______________________________

I will honor him: ______________________________

The original Hebrew words behind these phrases hold some surprises that can encourage you in your caregiving season. The God who promises to be with you in trouble is also the God who honors you for your faithfulness and courage. As you complete the following word study, call on God for understanding, and listen for all the ways he responds—sometimes unexpectedly.

Call (Hebrew *kawraw*)

This word can mean "to call out," "to address by name," "to cry," "to mention," or even "to accost." The idea of "accosting" God might surprise you. It means approaching him with persistence, even when the burden feels heavy. Jesus told a story about a widow who kept pestering a judge until he answered her plea (Luke 18:1–8). Like that widow, we are invited to keep calling out to God—to refuse to give up.

Write a brief description of a time when you found yourself repeatedly calling out to the Lord.

____

____

____

____

____

Answer (Hebrew *awnaw*)

This word means "to heed," "pay attention," "respond," "hear," "lift up," or "testify." God's answers to your calls may come in diverse ways—sometimes clearly, sometimes quietly. Certainly, he hears you.

Write down a few ways God has responded to your prayers during this caregiving season.

____

____

____

____

____

Trouble (Hebrew *tsawraw*)

This word means "tightness," "adversary," "adversity," "affliction," "anguish," "distress," or "tribulation." Like us, Old Testament believers faced many kinds of trouble.

List which of the definitions of trouble have been part of your caregiving journey.

____

____

____

____

____

Deliver (Hebrew *khawlats*)

This word suggests being rescued but also "pulling off," "equipping to fight," "drawing out," or "preparing." God is ready to help you shed burdens and obstacles that weigh you down.

Write down a burden you need God to pull off of you today.

____

____

____

____

____

Honor (Hebrew *kabad*)

This word means "to promote," "to glorify," "to make weighty, heavy, or rich." The presence of *kabad* in this promise from God is a beautiful surprise. In Job's story, God restored his wealth twofold, but honor isn't just about material blessings. The gift of *kabad* is about God lifting you up and valuing you deeply, even in the midst of hardship. Sometimes, this lifting up looks like a friend showing up unannounced with a meal, or a nurse calling you by name and asking how you are doing. In quiet, unexpected ways, God reminds you that you are not invisible—that your role matters and your heart is seen.

Write down at least one way God has honored you in your caregiving journey.

Caregiving can feel isolating. The invitation at Psalm 91:15 to call on God is an invitation to a relationship with him. Whether his response to your call comes gently, powerfully, or in surprising ways, it is certain to come.

Remember God's Faithfulness

Psalm 91:15 mentions one action we're asked to take and four promises God gives in return. Our one action is simple: to call on God. In response, God promises to answer us, to be with us in trouble, to rescue us, and to honor us. It certainly feels like we're receiving far more than we're giving. God's generous response to a call is a perfect example of his grace.

Why do we have to call on God if he already knows what we need? The reason is relationship. God doesn't just want to know about our struggles; he wants us to turn to him with trust. Calling on God is an invitation to partnership, a way of saying to God, "I believe you care about this trouble of mine, and I'm inviting you into its management." We can trust him in this partnership, even when we don't understand what's happening. Isaiah 55:8–9 gives us related insight into the mind of God.

> *"For my thoughts are not your thoughts, neither are your ways my ways," declares the Lord. "As the heavens are higher than the earth, so are my ways higher than your ways and my thoughts than your thoughts."*

During my caregiving years, I was often focused only on the next appointment, the next medication, the next decision. Later, I could see how God's purposes stretched far beyond each moment. Sometimes, his answers to our prayers came much later, in ways we didn't expect. Looking back, I can discern his fingerprints revealed in those years.

Can you see a greater purpose in your current trials? If not, that's okay. Ask God to help you glimpse what he's doing behind the scenes. Keep leaning into his promises, asking him for your needs, and trusting in his provision. The first book of John assures us that we can have total confidence in calling on God.

> *This is the confidence we have in approaching God: that if we ask anything according to his will, he hears us. (1 John 5:14)*

Write a short prayer inviting God's presence into your current situation, asking for his guidance regarding an immediate need, and entrusting that need to his care. If you don't know how to begin, use one of the prompts below.

"Lord, I call on you now because I need your help with . . ."

"Lord, help me trust that you know what is best, even if I can't see it yet."

____

____

____

____

____

From Linda's Journey

December 23, 2000

8:00 p.m.

"It doesn't feel much like Christmas," Allen says as he leaves for his last day of school before break. I have to agree.

I've done my best to create what cheer I could with an extremely limited budget, but without Ron's laughter in the house, a kind of gloom hangs over everything. A high fever last night kept Ron in the hospital for what the surgeon said would be "just one more day." I don't have much confidence, though, that my husband will be home for Christmas Eve.

As I leave for the middle school to teach my classes, I pass the empty corner of the living room where the Christmas tree should stand. We've only managed to put a simple strand of lights around the door outside. Bonnie and I just couldn't bring ourselves to do more. The hospital I visit daily has trees, garland, poinsettias. But forced cheer feels hollow.

At least we will be together, I remind myself. Dennis will be home from college, Bonnie's classes and the day care where she works are on break, and Allen has time off too. Even if Ron isn't home, we'll visit him and bring a little Christmas to his room.

That evening, we're sitting quietly in the living room, each lost in his or her own thoughts or activity, when there's a knock at the door. Allen peers through the window.

"It's a truck! Someone's coming up the walk!"

He flings the door open. "Wow! Is that for us?"

Rich and Rose, dear friends from church, stand on the porch holding a full, fragrant evergreen tree between them. Allen grabs a branch and helps drag it into the living room.

"How did you know we didn't have a tree?" Bonnie asks.

"We called Pastor Bill," Rose says with a smile. "He said you needed one."

Bonnie disappears to the attic for the tree ornaments we thought we wouldn't need. Allen runs to the basement for the tree stand. He and Rich set up the most beautiful tree I've ever seen. When they begin stringing the lights, Rose puts her arm around me.

"We saw Ron today," she says gently, reaching into her bag. "He asked me to get you this. It's from your husband."

She hands me a square red box topped with a white bow. Tears blur my vision, and I throw my arms around her.

Rose pats my shoulder. "I know, honey. I know."

Sometimes, I think, God shows his love through the kindness of others.

"Ta da!" says Allen when he plugs in the lights. The tree shimmers with red, white, and green twinkles that reflect in his eyes. "Now," he says, "it feels like Christmas."

Write down something your loved one has done—big or small—just to express "I love you."

____

____

____

____

____

Take a Moment

Psalm 91:15 reminds us that when we call on God, he not only answers but is with us in trouble, delivering and honoring us. As caregivers, it's comforting to remember that we are never alone and that God delights in responding to our calls. Reread Psalm 91:15 quietly, then write your responses to the questions.

> *He will call on me, and I will answer him; I will be with him in trouble, I will deliver him and honor him. (Psalm 91:15)*

1. How does knowing that God delights in you affect the way you call on him?

____

____

____

____

____

2. When have you experienced a surprising answer to prayer?

____

____

____

____

____

3. What is one way you can stay open to God's surprises in your caregiving journey?

____

____

____

____

____

Prayer for Calling on God

Dear God, thank you for always hearing my calls, even when I feel tired and unsure. Help me to keep reaching out to you, trusting that you are near and will answer in your perfect way. Teach me to expect surprises—those quiet moments of comfort, strength, and hope that remind me of your delight in me. In my caregiving journey, be my refuge and my guide. May I lean on you daily and rest in your faithful love. In Jesus' name, amen.

CHAPTER 12

Gaining More Than This Life

Verse for the Journey: With long life I will satisfy him and show him my salvation. (Psalm 91:16)

From Linda's Journey

January 11, 2001
8:00 p.m.

I'm standing behind a woman in the market tonight who buys a king-size Hershey bar and a *Good Housekeeping* magazine. I think to myself, *Good for you. Nothing like a little self-indulgence.* I don't know if both items are for her, but I like to imagine they're the beginning of an evening of rest and self-care.

No offense intended, but she looks like she could use a little self-care. Tired. Drawn. Winter has stolen the life from her hair and left her skin pale.

She looks a lot like me.

I'm here, grabbing a few things after visiting Ron at the hospital. There's no Hershey bar in my future. One might make a nice accompaniment to the papers in my book bag that need grading by tomorrow, but just one bar wouldn't last through those, plus the six chapters in a graduate school text I must read by Monday.

Don't focus on the temporary, I think as I pay for my purchases. *Focus on the eternal.*

Ron is slowly recovering from the latest surgery, completed three days ago. The recovery has been painful for him. When I saw him today, though, his eyes sparkled with a light I thought I would never see again. He laughed more and delighted in putting his chilly hands on my neck to make me shriek. Both his body and his spirit are healing.

No matter what the future holds for Ron's body, God's rewards in a healed spirit are eternal. And that's what I'm living to witness in Ron and experience in myself.

Rest in God's Protection

The long life mentioned in Psalm 91:16 does not mean we will all reach a ripe old age. This earthly life is temporary, fragile, and sometimes painfully short. God's promise becomes clearer in the second part of the verse: "I will show him my salvation." The long life

God promises is much bigger than birthdays. It's life in relationship with him, life that starts here and lasts forever.

The Hebrew word for "salvation" in this verse is rich with meaning. According to Strong's Concordance, it also means "deliverance." Our salvation will deliver us from sin, fear, and, ultimately, death itself. There is much more to our salvation than our final destiny. Salvation is God's active work in our lives right now. His promises for protection, healing, rescue, provision, and peace belong to us today, in the middle of any mess we may be experiencing.

Choosing from God's promises of protection, healing, rescue, provision, and peace, write down the promises you see evidenced in your life now.

____

____

____

____

____

Psalm 91:16 says God will show us our salvation. We don't have to wait until we get to heaven to experience God's goodness. We get to see God's work here and now. He gives us comfort when we grieve, unexpected provision, and peace that makes no sense to many in the world.

Seeing evidence of our salvation does not mean life will be easy. We will face many obstacles, but God can lead us away from dangers and anxieties that come with careless choices. Proverbs 1:7 tells us to pay attention to instruction.

> *The fear of the Lord is the beginning of knowledge, but fools despise wisdom and instruction.*

Those who follow godly wisdom are not immune from harm but are less likely to suffer it, as they are led to avoid risky activities, unhealthy habits, and anxiety. Paul explained that the knowledge of our salvation encourages wise choices.

> *Do you not know that your bodies are temples of the Holy Spirit, who is in you, whom you have received from God? You are not your own; you were bought at a price. Therefore, honor God with your bodies. (1 Corinthians 6:19–20)*

Taking care of ourselves is a way we honor God. Write one way you can follow Godly wisdom today by practicing self-care.

____

____

____

____

____

Our life on earth will end. The Bible assures us that for those who trust in Christ, death brings us into the immediate presence of God.

> *We are confident, I say, and would prefer to be away from the body and at home with the Lord. (2 Corinthians 5:8).*

That's the hope I cling to.

When my husband fell asleep in his easy chair on July 13, 2019, he found himself in heaven. His many years of battle with a failing body were over. I have tried to imagine what it was like for Ron to wake up in God's presence.

Write down what you think it might be like to wake up in the presence of God.

____

____

____

____

____

Renew Through God's Word

The biblical Abraham died "in a good old age, an old man and full of years" (Genesis 25:8). God promised long earthly life to Abraham's descendants, the people of Israel, with a stipulation.

Honor your father and your mother, so that you may live long in the land the Lord your God is giving you. (Exodus 20:12)

Psalm 91:16, God promises a long life that is about more than physical years. He says, "With long life I will satisfy him and show him my salvation." God doesn't just want us to live long; he wants us to live satisfied.

Write a few thoughts about what a satisfied life would look like to you.

____

____

____

____

____

The word *satisfy* means to fill with contentment and purpose. God doesn't want you to merely exist, worn out and discouraged. He wants you to find fulfillment and purpose, even in the hard seasons. Caregiving often brings moments of emptiness. Plans can be delayed, dreams put on pause, and friendships strained.

Write down a need or disappointment to bring honestly before God, who promises you a satisfied life.

The Hebrew word translated "salvation" in Psalm 91:16 is the Hebrew name of Jesus, *Yeshua*. That word also refers to health, healing, prosperity, victory, deliverance, rescue, safety, and protection. Salvation is both a present reality and a future hope.

You might not feel "saved" in the sense of being rescued from your circumstances. You might still feel surrounded by uncertainty or fear. Maybe the sense of safety you used to feel with your spouse seems distant now. Psalm 91 reminds us that true safety comes not from other people but from belonging to God.

One of God's names is Jehovah Nissi, meaning "The Lord Is my Banner" (Exodus 17:15). This name first appears after a battle in which God gave victory to his people. Moses built an altar and named it Jehovah Nissi, as a sign of God's covering.

A banner waving over an army marks the soldiers' identity, unity, and protection. When we call on God as Jehovah Nissi, we are acknowledging God's leadership and authority. We are trusting him to go before us.

Knowing God paves the way before us matters deeply to a caregiver. When you feel that life is a battlefield of emotions, decisions, and exhaustion, recall that God is waving his banner over you. He has claimed you as his own.

Write here what you imagine the banner God has over you might say.

____

____

____

____

____

Remember God's Faithfulness

During the many times Ron was in the hospital, Allen kept a hammer under his mattress, a small and tangible way he could protect his "girls" from dangers in the night. In reality, our true protection comes not from a hammer or other potential weapon but from God, who is described at Proverbs 18:10 as a "strong tower." As expressed by Psalm 4:8, trusting in God's promises about safety and refuge can help us find rest and peace in him alone, even in the hardest trials.

In peace I will lie down and sleep, for you alone, Lord, make me dwell in safety.

Briefly describe a time when you now know God protected you from harm.

God's protection includes his provision. After Ron's car accident, God provided for my family in many practical ways—through money from friends or coworkers, meals from church members, and even a Christmas tree. These provisions were tangible signs of God's ongoing care.

Write down a few ways God has made provisions for you or your family during this season of caregiving.

Caregiving can be exhausting and taking care of your own health while caregiving might feel impossible. But God calls us to honor him by caring for our bodies, the temples of the Holy Spirit (1 Corinthians 6:19–20). I implemented and recommend three simple self-care behaviors.

1. Rest when you can. I spent many nights at the hospital, but I gradually learned that my presence there wasn't necessary. The medical professionals on staff could manage any situation, and the kind nurses promised to call me if I was needed.
2. Exercise now and then. Sitting in a stiff chair in a waiting room is not comfortable. I made it a habit to walk around the hospital every half hour. Movement will clear your head and strengthen your body. One hospital had a lovely atrium to walk through. Even if you're just walking in the halls, you're getting some exercise.
3. Eat as healthily as you can. Hospital food may not offer gourmet choices, but you can usually find salads and fruit. I found that when I got to know food service workers and shared my preference for tuna salad, they saved a serving for me.

Write down which of the three simple self-care behaviors you especially need to focus on today.

____

____

____

____

____

From Linda's Journey

March 3, 2001

5:00 p.m.

It began here, in this hospital corridor. I have timed the trip down this passage, sometimes making a game out of it, trying to improve my pace. This will be, I pray, the last time we make this trek, which has been part of our lives for a year.

Each member of my family walks slowly, lost in his or her own thoughts. Bonnie, recovering from a recent kidney infection, walks as slowly as her father, who leans heavily on his walker. Our oldest son, Dennis, has joined us today. We are a family that has survived a long and difficult journey together.

The walls and the carpeting are familiar, as are many of the faces we pass. I recognize fellow travelers on their own health journeys, even if I do not know their names. I've sat in waiting rooms with them, sipping hot beverages from foam cups. I have prayed with them. I have cried with them.

We reach the lobby. The same burgundy and green furniture sits on the same beige rugs. There are touches of green today in honor of the approaching Irish holiday. I have seen this lobby decked out for Easter, Halloween, Thanksgiving, Christmas, and Valentine's Day. The seasons have passed during our sojourn through Ron's recovery.

The surgical unit is to our left, just beyond the bank of elevators. It is our first stop. We deposit the flowers we have brought to the nurses who cared for Ron. There are quick hugs and handshakes. We do not linger but soon head up to the fourth floor. We have more units to visit, more flowers to deliver, more hugs to give and receive. Eventually, we circle back down to the lobby. The kids stay with their father while I get the car.

Ron is coming home to stay. Slowly, step by step, we have come to the end of this part of the recovery journey. We have all been changed by it. I know in my heart that my journey as a caregiver will continue. There is no going back to life without the shadow and lingering effects of all the related trials on our hearts.

For now, I can rejoice in the excellent care Ron has received and in his homecoming. God has sheltered us in his wings, provided refuge in times of uncertainty, and listened to our calls. I don't know what the future holds for any of us, but I can taste the satisfaction of God's promises—peace, presence, and purpose in the middle of pain.

Take a Moment

Psalm 91:16 promises long life, but that doesn't mean we will avoid sickness and live to an old age. Instead, it means that our eternity in heaven is safe.

There, all illnesses and injuries will be healed. Reread the verse, then write your responses to the questions that follow.

With long life I will satisfy him and show him my salvation. (Psalm 91:16)

1. What does it mean to you that God's promise of long life is about satisfaction and relationship, not just the number of your years?

2. In what specific ways have you seen God's salvation—his help, provision, or rescue—during your caregiving journey?

3. How can trusting in God's promises help you rest in him today, even if your caregiving journey is not yet over?

Prayer for Salvation Strength

Lord, thank you for the gift of salvation—not just for eternity, but for every day I walk this caregiving journey. You cover me with your banner of love and meet me with provision, peace, and unexpected joy. Teach me to live a life that is not only long but satisfied in you. When I feel weary or unsure, remind me that your salvation is both my strength today and my hope forever. Help me trust you, step by step. May I rest in your faithful presence today. In Jesus' name, amen

Benediction from Linda

Whether you are just stepping into the role of spousal caregiver or already deep in the journey, I want you to know you are not invisible. You are visible and never alone. Your tears, your fatigue, and your prayers in the quiet hours matter. They are seen by God, who promises to shelter you under his wings.

I was a spousal caregiver for nineteen years. That journey was long, often exhausting, and filled with moments of grief, doubt, and heartache. There were days when I had nothing left to give, when hope seemed distant, strength hard to find. But even in the hardest moments, God's faithfulness met me. His shelter was real. His protection was not always the kind I expected, but it was always exactly what I needed. He is ready to give the protection you need.

The years after my husband's accident were not the life we had planned to have together, but they were precious years, full of unexpected joys and hard-won victories. I am grateful for every moment we shared, extra time beyond the scene of the accident. Through it all, God sustained us and our family—not just physically, but spiritually and emotionally. He will sustain you, too.

Let caring for your own heart and health be an essential part of your caregiving life. Don't be afraid to lean on others for help, and never hesitate to lean fully on God. There is no shame in feeling weary. There is only grace offered anew each morning.

My prayer is that this guided study has wrapped you in the truth of God's promises and reminded you that even in the hardest times, he is your refuge and strength. Keep walking in his care, dear one. You are braver and stronger than you know. You are held in everlasting arms.

If you're interested in continuing your caregiving journey in community with other caregivers, I invite you to connect with me through my blog at lindaca1.substack.com, where you'll find ongoing encouragement, as well as information about an online support group and a monthly podcast for caregivers.

Walk forward in grace, under the shelter of God's wings.

Prayer for the Journey Ahead

Heavenly Father, thank you for walking with me through the difficulties of caregiving. Thank you for your promises of protection, peace, and strength. Please continue to guide my steps and fill my heart with courage and hope. Help me rest in your presence, knowing that I am never alone. Help me dwell in your shelter and take cover under your wings. Bless all who are on a caregiving journey and remind us daily of your unchanging love. In Jesus' name, amen.

Bible Verse Index

Verses have been referenced from the Blue Letter Bible/ New International Version unless otherwise noted.

Invisible but Never Alone

Galatians 6:9

2 Corinthians 4:16–17

God's Psalm 91 Promises for You

Psalm 91

Chapter 1. Sheltering in God's Shadow

Psalm 27:5

Isaiah 32:2

Song of Solomon 2:3

Psalm 63:7

Isaiah 49:2

Romans 8:35

Romans 8:28

John 14:27

Chapter 2. Building Trust While in Refuge

2 Peter 1:19

Ruth 1:16

John 20:25

Matthew 27:46

Genesis 50:20

Chapter 3. Remaining Safe in God's Care

Psalm 121:7–8

Psalm 124:7

1 John 2:16

Psalm 91:3 KJV

Hebrews 13:8

John 3:16

Chapter 4. Receiving the Covering of God's Faithfulness

Psalm 31:20

Psalm 27:5

Isaiah 32:2

Ruth 2:12

Psalm 91:4 KJV

Chapter 5. Braving the Night

Isaiah 26:3

Philippians 4:6–7

Ephesians 3:16–18

1 John 4:4

Luke 12:32

Mark 4:40

Hebrews 7:20–22

Chapter 6. Staying Beside God

Psalm 34:7

John 16:33

1 Timothy 2:1–4

Psalm 7:16

Isaiah 43:1

Chapter 7. Dwelling with the Most High

Luke 21:34 KJV

Psalm 90:1

Psalm 84:1–2

Psalm 31:20

2 Corinthians 5:1

Chapter 8. Inviting Angel Guardians

Job 38:4–7

Hebrews 13:2

Daniel 9:20–22

1 Kings 19:5–6

Acts 12:7–8

Matthew 4:11

Psalm 103:20

Isaiah 6:2–3

2 Thessalonians 1:6–7

Chapter 9. Treading on Trouble

Isaiah 26:3

Romans 8:37

Romans 16:20

Revelation 12:9
Luke 10:17–20
John 14:12
Matthew 17:20
Romans 8:18
Romans 5:3–4
Philippians 3:21
Hebrews 13:8

Chapter 10. Finding Courage in God's Rescue

Deuteronomy 31:8
Isaiah 40:29
2 Timothy 4:18
John 3:16–18
Proverbs 3:5–6
1 John 4:4
Romans 12:2
Habakkuk 3:17–18
1 Peter 5:7
John 8:29

Chapter 11. Calling on God for Answers

Matthew 2:11
John 16:33
Psalm 18:17–19
Romans 8:28
2 Corinthians 1:4
Isaiah 55:8–9
I John 5:14

Chapter 12. Gaining More Than This Life

Proverbs 1:7

1 Corinthians 6:19–20

2 Corinthians 5:8

Genesis 25:8

Exodus 20:12

Exodus 17:15

Proverbs 18:10

Psalm 4:8